THE DARK FACE OF SCIENCE

By the same Author

THE SHAKESPEAREAN ETHIC
SHAKESPEARE AND THE ROSE OF LOVE
SHAKESPEARE AND PLATONIC BEAUTY
A CASE AGAINST JONES:
A Study of Psychical Phenomena
IN PITY AND IN ANGER

The Tools of Science

THE DARK FACE OF SCIENCE

John Vyvyan

LONDON
MICHAEL JOSEPH

First published in Great Britain by
MICHAEL JOSEPH LTD
*52 Bedford Square
London, W.C.1*
1971

© 1971 by John Vyvyan

All Rights Reserved. No part of this publication may be reproduced, stored in a retrieval system, or transmitted, in any form or by any means, electronic, mechanical, photocopying, recording or otherwise, without the prior permission of the Copyright owner

7181 0879 5

Set and printed in Great Britain by Tonbridge Printers Ltd, Peach Hall Works, Tonbridge, Kent, in Bembo twelve on fourteen point, on paper supplied by P. F. Bingham Ltd, and bound by James Burn at Esher, Surrey

To the memory of Miss Netta Ivory of Edinburgh, who, with her sister, founded the Scottish Society for the Prevention of Vivisection, and throughout her life devoted her great gifts of heart and mind to this cause.

AUTHOR'S NOTE

I do not think the title of this book will be misunderstood, but I should like to guard against that possibility. I love science. I owe to it a new understanding of the world, and a deeper satisfaction in existence. *La joie de connaitre* is a joy that I have felt and would wish to share. But there is, none the less, a dark face to science. And my efforts to dispel that darkness are a measure of my love.

CONTENTS

List of illustrations   11

Acknowledgements   13

1. 1900   17
2. Bernard Shaw and the Girls from Sweden   24
3. *The Shambles of Science*   35
4. The Hon. Stephen Coleridge   48
5. The Brown-Dog Riots   59
6. The Second Royal Commission   66
7. Walter Robert Hadwen   80
8. The World Schism   89
9. *La Grande Morale*   103
10. The Science of Death   112
11. The New Sowers   118
12. The Puppet-Players   127
13. John Cowper Powys   138
14. The Myth of *Morwyn*   144

CONTENTS

15	The Explosion	155
16	A New Vision of Life	172
17	The World Problem and the Grounds of Protest	180
	Appendix	198
	Index	205

ILLUSTRATIONS

1	The Tools of Science	*frontispiece*	
2	Bernard Shaw in the 1890's	*facing page*	64
3	Louise Lind-af-Hageby		65
4	The Hon. Stephen Coleridge		96
5	Harvey Metcalfe		97
6	Air Chief Marshal Lord Dowding		160
7	Professor S. T. Aygün		161

ACKNOWLEDGEMENTS

I should like to express my thanks to Professor S. T. Aygün of the University of Ankara for permitting me to use extracts from two of his addresses as an Appendix to this book, to Mr Harvey Metcalfe of the Scottish Society for the Prevention of Vivisection, to Mrs Muriel Hort, Librarian of the Lawson Tait Memorial Trust, to Mr Charles Slatter and Mr Colin Smith of the National Anti-Vivisection Society, to Mr John Pitt, editor of *The Anti-Vivisection Times*, and to Hon. George R. Farnum of the New England Anti-Vivisection Society, all of whom have given me generous help.

For permission to reproduce photographs, my thanks are due to the Presbyterian College of Florida, *frontispiece;* Messrs William Collins & Co., 2; the Animal-Defence and Anti-Vivisection Society, 3; The Lord Coleridge, c.b.e., 4; Mr Harvey Metcalfe, 5; the Rt Hon. Muriel, Lady Dowding, 6; the International Association against Painful Experiments on Animals, 7.

Le souffle de la science moderne, qui anime la physiologie, est éminemment conquérant et dominateur.

The spirit of modern science, which inspires physiology, is pre-eminently one of conquest and of domination.

CLAUDE BERNARD

Weh! Weh!
Du hast sie zerstört,
Die schöne Welt,
Mit mächtiger Faust;
Sie stürzt, sie zerfällt!
Ein Halbgott hat sie zerschlagen!

Woe! woe! you have shattered it, the beautiful world, with your mighty fist. It reels, it falls, stricken by a half-god!

GOETHE

CHAPTER ONE

1900

'The first day of the new century sees our army – in other words, our people in arms – gathered around their standards, kneeling before the Lord of Hosts.'

The speaker was the German Emperor, and the ceremony was a rededication of regimental flags. Ostensibly, this was an act of Christian worship: effectively, it was an evocation and an exaltation of the spirit of violence. The Emperor had a talent for oratory, and surely none of the countless speeches made on that New Year's Day can have proved more apt to the coming era.

Armies kneeling before the Lord of Hosts, and a world to be broken by his rod of iron.

Nothing so portentious was being said in England. The Queen was at Osborne, but she had no rousing message to give. Her era was over. The correspondence columns of *The Times*, on the first of January 1900, were filled with letters debating the question of whether the twentieth century had in fact begun. Some argued that this would not happen for another twelve months, while others were no less certain that on that Monday morning, when the familiar 18' changed to the strange 19', the world had entered on a new age. No doubt the latter were right; for a century is not only a question of arithmetic, it is also a state of mind.

As the eighteen-hundreds drew to a close, even the lightest minds were stirred to thought; and almost everyone who could use a pen recorded something of his reflections and his prophecies. A fascinating anthology might now be made from these dreams and guesses. For the most part, they were optimistic and did not foresee the clouds of poison-gas, the devastated cities, and the prison-camps of torture and degradation that were to come. But one thing that nobody could fail to notice was the progress of Science, and the advent of Scientific Man. Here, it was evident to all, there was a new power in the world. Would this also serve the cults of violence?

Some years earlier, Claude Bernard had defined the spirit of modern science as one of conquest and of domination. '*Le souffle de la science moderne, qui anime la physiologie, est éminemment conquérant et dominateur.*' There are, of course, noble conquests; and neither the Kaiser nor Claude Bernard was bereft of good qualities. But each, in his own way, had announced and exalted a theme of violence. These were not unrelated; and they form, as it were, the background and the foreground of this book. Psychopathic aggression has become the characteristic social sickness of our time; and the spectacular increase in the ill-use of animals in science – an increase throughout the world from some thousands annually to uncounted millions – is one aspect of this complex evil. Even some of those who are engaged in it will not deny that it is intrinsically an evil. And the story of the anti-vivisection movement in the twentieth century, which we have now to tell, is that of a spontaneous effort at self-healing by a sick society.

Among those who, when the century opened, were contemplating the future with reasonable, but not immoderate hope was an American doctor of medicine, Albert Leffingwell. He was mainly concerned with the deeper sorts of change; and he observed that the turn of the century coincided with one of the greatest, perhaps the very greatest turning-point in human thought.

'We are almost at the beginning of the twentieth century', he wrote. 'Civilization is about to enter a new era, with new problems to solve, new dangers to confront, new hopes to realize. It is useless to deny the increasing ascendancy of that spirit which in regard to the problems of the universe affirms nothing, denies nothing, but continues its search for a solution; it is equally useless to shut our eyes to the influence of this spirit upon those beliefs which for many ages have anchored human conduct to ethical ideals. Regret would be futile; and here, perhaps, is no occasion for regret. . . . But all real progress in civilization depends upon man's ethical ideals . . .

'Within the lifetime of most of us, has not science invested this whole question with a new aspect? For eighteen centuries of Christian civilization the wisest and best of mankind regarded the under-world of animated nature as beings not only different from ourselves, but infinitely beneath us in origin and destiny. Now modern science has promulgated a new doctrine. No theory is more firmly held by biologists today than that hypothesis of Darwin which derives from the same far-distant ancestry both animals and man . . . "There was a time when even your ancestors, O professor of biology, and those of the dog beneath your knife, were of the same species of living creatures," speaks the science of today. "Out of the same black darkness, struggling for existence, you have emerged – in far different form, but yet closely related, not only by origin but in every function of organized existence. That quivering nerve acts precisely as your nerves would behave under like excitation, and it will feel the same anguish yours would feel. That brain you are about to penetrate, hides in some infinitely mysterious way the germs of mind; the elements, at least, of intelligence, obedience, reverence, contrition, faithfulness and unselfish affection. Ah, sir! your keenest knife cannot lay bare these mysteries." So much, indeed, Science may tell us. 'These despised beings are your kindred," she asserts. Whether our conduct towards them is right or wrong is a question beyond her province to decide.'*

Here Leffingwell laid his finger on the fundamental change which makes the twentieth century different from every other –

---

* Albert Leffingwell: *The Vivisection Controversy*, English ed., 1908, pp. 52, 59–60.

the new knowledge of man's place in nature. Nearly all the arguments against cruelty to animals in the nineteenth century turned ultimately on some theological statement about our duty to God's creatures; but now they derive their force increasingly from a new conception – our duty to the simpler members of our own family. 'The plea of the humanitarian,' Bernard Shaw wrote, 'is a plea for widening the range of fellow-feeling.' This is far more intimate and compelling. It is possible for a theologian to maintain that animals have no feelings, no intelligence, and were created solely for man's use; but it is not possible for a scientist to do so. No one who has even a rudimentary education in science can reject evolution or deny the implications of cousinship.

We are therefore confronted with this new fact, which makes it necessary to re-think our ethics. Science cannot dictate our ethics; but it would be untrue to say that it has none of its own, for it is obliged to acknowledge at least one commandment, '*Thou shalt not twist the facts*'. Casuistry, obscurantism and mendacity are 'sins' against science, because they are contrary to its nature and impede its progress; and the ethic of science might, perhaps, be summed up by saying that what advances science is right and what retards it is wrong. This is proper within limits; but when scientists go on to assert or to imply, as they often have done, that any legal measure that might impede science is necessarily wrong, the limits have been over-stepped.

The public does not usually notice this transgression. It has been so dazzled by the shining face of science that it finds the dark one difficult to discern. The sinister face and the over-stepping were well exemplified, however, by another American writer near the turn of the century. E. E. Slosson was professor of chemistry at one of the state universities; and on the threshold of the new era, his words stand in ominous contrast to those of Leffingwell. In an article, *The Relative Value of Life and Learning*, which appeared in *The Independent* of New York, Professor Slosson wrote:

'Is science worth the cost? Is a life for a line too high a price to pay for additions to our knowledge? No one who knows the value of learning would say it is. On the contrary . . . a human life is nothing compared with a new fact . . . the aim of science is the advancement of human knowledge at any sacrifice of human life.

'If cats and guinea pigs can be put to any higher use than to advance science, we do not know what it is. We do not know of any higher use we can put a man to . . . If it were necessary to kill a dozen cats to impress on the mind of one pupil the workings of the mammalian heart, no true teacher would hesitate to do it; and whether it is necessary only the teacher can decide.'*

These conclusions were arrived at with much show of reason – one can find reasons for anything – and if some readers of *The Independent* demurred to them, it will not have been because the argument was unimpressive. None the less, a teacher who holds these views is a dangerous man: his pupils may become more learned, but they will not grow better under his instruction. The objection that thus to exhibit the workings of a cat's heart might damage the finer feelings of a human heart would have seemed unscientific to the professor. So indeed it is; but it is not, therefore, irrelevant. Civilization is much concerned with finer feelings, and it may even depend on them. We have been encouraged to believe that what adds to science adds to human good; but if this is true, it is only by virtue of our finer feelings. Whatever advances science undoubtedly advances human power, but it is not impossible that scientists may be piling up knowledge for criminals to explode. If our race should meet with destruction, it will not be due to an 'act of God' but to an act of Scientific Man; and to frame our laws so that the pursuit of knowledge is made exempt from the restraints of mercy may be to invite catastrophy.

Nobody doubts that there are dangers in the misuse of knowledge, but some people will deny that there are also dangers in its

* 12 December, 1895.

misacquisition. Aldous Huxley wrote a book to establish the proposition that means condition ends, or, as he put it, that 'the end cannot justify the means, for the simple and obvious reason that the means employed determine the nature of the ends produced.'*
If this had been simple and obvious – unfortunately it is not – it would never have been supposed that socially desirable ends could be achieved by cruel methods; it would have been evident that the people who employ such methods will themselves be conditioned by them in ways that they neither desire nor expect; and that insofar as the great institutions of science lend their support to cruel procedures, they are making cruelty acceptable to society. This is not an end at which they aim, for it amounts to barbarization; but it is one that Huxley's argument predicts.

In *Ends and Means*, Huxley also made an assumption: 'Real progress,' he maintained, 'is progress in charity, all other advances being secondary thereto.' Judged by that criterion, and with reference only to human relations, he considered that we were in regression. But even if he were mistaken, is the human sphere enough to judge by? How wide is charity? In his later writings, Huxley advanced an organic view of nature. Ecologically – and, one may think, psychically – the world is an organism. Its welfare depends on mutually-beneficient interaction between its parts. We are only one part of nature; and we cannot abuse the rest and ourselves prosper – or even survive.

Many people, of course, will deny that charity is the measure of human progress. What, then, will they affirm? What is the standard of an advancing civilization? When we put this question to our academies of science, their effective answer is that of Claude Bernard – that the standard is one of conquest and of domination. It need scarcely be said that science as such is unsullied by these passions; its pursuit could be among the purest of our joys, and its attainments among the finest of our satisfactions; but Bernard

* Aldous Huxley: *Ends and Means*, 1938, p. 9. Reproduced here by kind permission of Chatto & Windus Ltd, and Mrs Laura Huxley.

described correctly a ruthless quality in himself, and in his successors, which has found expression in cruelties without parallel, and has made science in this century the strong arm of the wider cults of violence. In this spirit, we have been striving to create the world we want; and twice within living memory, we have achieved a blood-drenched chaos.

CHAPTER TWO

Bernard Shaw and the Girls from Sweden

The month of May 1900 is memorable in the literary history of the anti-vivisection movement on account of two addresses by Bernard Shaw. On the twenty-second of May, he spoke to the National Anti-Vivisection Society in Queen's Hall, and on the thirtieth, to the London Anti-Vivisection Society. Shaw's enthusiasm was for the cause itself, and he gave his support impartially to any organization by which he thought it might be advanced.

Most of his plays had not then been written, but Shaw himself was never more exuberant than at the opening of the century. He was one of the most sought-after speakers in England. He did not take money for his lectures, and spoke only on subjects that he desired to further. If he spoke in the provinces, his fee was a third-class return ticket; and he was prepared to address any kind of audience from any kind of foothold, from an up-turned orange-box at a street-corner to the secure platform of the British Association for the Advancement of Science. Although he did this without pecuniary reward, wherever he spoke the money flowed in; and it is said that some of the smaller socialist societies, then existing on a shoe-string, were able to balance their budgets for several years from one Shaw lecture.

In the summer of 1900, he was engaged in writing the preface to *Three Plays for Puritans*. One of these was *Caesar and Cleopatra*, and the preface contains the notorious section, *Better than Shakespeare?* Few people then living can have been more self-confident, or have had better reason to be; but beneath the stylist and the entertainer, sometimes delighting and sometimes infuriating, Shaw was a great humanitarian, who really believed in 'the holiness of life'. And it was therefore inevitable that he should speak against the cruelties of science.

By 1900 the anti-vivisection movement had been in organized existence for a quarter of a century in England, and it had received the support of most of the great Victorians – Tennyson, Browning, Carlyle and Ruskin among them. But it never had a more dazzling advocate than Shaw. Others wrote finely, as one might expect; but only Shaw, who was no less serious than any of them, has made the movement laugh. This was a valuable service, which he continued to render until the end of his life. The method of the court-jester, the philosopher in cap and bells, has sometimes proved effectual in other spheres; but on this particular subject one might have thought it impossible to be entertaining without breach of taste. And the fact that Shaw could be so, despite the depth of his own feelings, is not the least of his achievements.

The May lectures were not the beginning of his advocacy. Some years earlier, Frances Cobbe, the foundress of both the National Anti-Vivisection Society and the British Union for the Abolition of Vivisection, had published a book which contained one or two inaccuracies, and Victor Horsley, Professor of Physiology at University College, had accused her publicly of telling lies. Shaw had then sprung to her defence:

'I at once took the field against Horsley. "The question at issue," I said, "is not whether Miss Cobbe is a liar, but whether you as a vivisector are a scoundrel." Horsley's breath was taken away. He refused to debate what seemed to him a monstrous insult...

'I defined a scoundrel as a person who pursued his aims and interests without regard to common morality or any of the restraints of civilization. The vivisector, I declared, is actually the worst of scoundrels, a scoundrel on principle; for no thief or murderer attempts to justify theft or murder as such, and claims not only impunity but respect and protection for them...

'I claimed nothing more than that the pursuit of knowledge should be subject to the same civilized morality and legality as any other activity.'*

Horsley seems to have enjoyed denouncing 'Miss Cobbe and her lying crew'; but Shaw's retort struck him as ill-mannered; and when challenged to a public debate, he declined. This is to be regretted, for it would have been a memorable encounter. Horsley could be adroit in argument: when the case required, he could be truthful; when insult would be effective, he could be insulting; and when twisting seemed desirable, he could bamboozle and twist. The London correspondent of *The New York Times* once paid a visit to his laboratory, and afterwards wrote an article on the happiness of the animals he had seen there. He mentioned in particular some monkeys – 'quite unaffected by the removal of a spinal cord'. As he might as well have written 'unaffected by the removal of their heads', one must suppose that the professor who had shown him round had a sense of humour. A public debate between Shaw and Horsley would certainly have been memorable, and it might even have added something to English literature.

To a modest extent, the May lectures did do that; and they also made a contribution to humanitarian thought. Shaw stressed the same points on both occasions, although he worded them differently. Some of these points are still relevant, and it would be difficult to state them better.

'Now, ladies and gentlemen, I am very well aware of the fact that the majority of doctors defend vivisection; but I am glad to say that the majority of them do not know what they are defend-

* *Shaw on Vivisection*, Allen & Unwin, 1949, 'Looking Backward.'

ing. I assure you that the average practitioner knows nothing of the horrors of the physiological laboratory, and is incapable of performing the experiments of which he considers himself bound to be the defender. I have myself been lectured by a doctor for my folly and ignorance on the subject of vivisection. I replied by describing a typical and highly interesting experiment to him and asked him what he thought of that. He broke out into expressions of disgust, and even went to the anti-humanitarian extreme of declaring that the man who did it deserved to be hanged.'

The charge of ignorance is made so often against the anti-vivisectionist that it is refreshing – and just – to find it reversed. The screen of secrecy and silence behind which these activities are sheltered has made some measure of ignorance inevitable; and there are also – on both sides – some shuttered minds. Many people who oppose vivisection have undoubtedly persuaded themselves of a number of questionable 'truths'. One of these is that vivisection is medically useless. Only a time-wasting, barren argument can come from defending this; and, as Shaw pointed out, it is in any case no firm ground on which to fight.

'If you abandon the dogmatic humanitarian attitude, if you say that this is a question which has to be decided by the benefit the practice confers or may confer, then you put yourself hopelessly in the wrong. As you know, we who are on the anti-vivisection side have cited case after case in which the experiments of the vivisectors have not led to the results claimed for them. Now I myself attach a great deal of value to demonstrations of that kind. They throw a great deal of light on the psychology of cruelty and credulity: they have all sorts of interest. But they are not conclusive to me in any way as arguments against vivisection. This for two reasons. First, if you attempt to controvert a vivisectionist by showing that the experiment he has performed has not led to any useful result, you imply that if it had led to a useful result you would consider his experiment justified. Now, I am not prepared to concede that position.

'The second reason is that although you may succeed in proving that none of the experiments hitherto tried has benefited anybody ... you are still in the position that for all you can prove, an experiment may be performed tomorrow which will directly or accidentally add to the sum of human knowledge and confer a benefit on humanity.' *May 22.*

'For my part, I must confess to you at once that I do not believe that any experiment can be tried in this world that may not be of some use to somebody or other, or that may not lead to some discovery. I have never objected to experiments on the ground that they are useless. ... Therefore, even if I were qualified professionally to do so, I do not think I should take my stand here tonight on the uselessness of vivisection. Nothing can be proved to be useless.

'You do not settle whether an experiment is justified or not by merely showing that it is of some use ... for surely, if a doctor believes that vivisectional experiments on animals are justified by what they teach him, then, since he knows that these must necessarily be less instructive than experiments on human beings, he must be a coward if he does not sacrifice one or two comparatively valueless human beings in order to find out a little more accurately what he is trying to discover.' *May 30.*

'I suggest to you, ladies and gentlemen, that if you bring this home to the ordinary man, he will see that it leads him much further than he desires to go ... He must draw the line somewhere; and if he draws it in such a way as to include quadrupeds only, the doctor may draw it a little higher up. He may say, quite logically, 'Here is a person who will never be missed. If I perform an experiment on him in the interest of science, and anything comes of it, that man by his death under my scalpel will have done more for the world than if I had merely cured him.' *May 22.*

'You see you cannot bring a thing of this kind to a utilitarian test at all. If you once begin that particular line of argument, you will find yourself landed in horrors of which you have no conception.' *May 30.*

The place to draw the line, then, is not between quadrupeds and bipeds, but between civilized and barbarous behaviour; and the real argument is not over animal species, but over human conduct.

'We must', Shaw insisted, 'apply the test of character, and ask ourselves not merely, "What will happen if I do this particular thing?" but, "What sort of a man shall I be if I do it?" I make no pretence to criticize vivisection-experiments on grounds of their technical failure or success. I dogmatically postulate humaneness as a condition of worthy personal character.' *May 30.*

Shaw raised a good deal of laughter at these two meetings; and they afford an excellent example of the Shavian method, which was to entertain people in order to persuade them to listen to things they did not wish to be told. He himself was never more serious than when, at the second of them, he delighted his audience by drawing a parallel between the advancement of science and social reform. He declared himself to be strongly in favour of social reform – but not by any method. And he went on to describe the tragic death of a fellow revolutionary, whose means of social reform exploded in his pocket. His means was dynamite. And Shaw entitled this lecture, *The Dynamitards of Science.*

* * *

The occasional contributions of brilliant men have never been wanting to this movement; but if a cause is to be advanced effectively, it requires also a certain number of people who will devote their lives to it. 'Dedicate their lives to it' would not be too much to say of this cause; because no material reward is to be expected from fighting against abuses that the public in the main accepts. If governments pay attention to such reformers, it is merely to impede them. Their work will bring neither fortunes nor honours, nor, very likely, much obvious success. In spite of this, the anti-vivisection movement has never lacked the service of talented men and women who might have had all these things if they had chosen to employ their gifts in other fields. Why, one may ask, did they take up, and never relinquish, this arduous, heart-breaking task?

Sometimes it has been because the so-called 'dumb' made themselves understood, and by a look or cry of anguish awakened pity, the conviction of injustice, and the sense of shame. Those who responded to this appeal have received no public thanks, but they have done something to redeem the honour of the human race. At times, they have behaved unwisely; they have often quarrelled among themselves; they have been fighters rather than saints; and their errors are on record. But they will none the less be remembered, if our world does not go down in chaos, because their endeavour to uphold the claims of mercy is of more real value than our pitiless achievement.

Among those who joined the movement at the beginning of the century were two Swedish girls. Although they had known each other since childhood, their friendship was then recent. It had begun one evening at the Opera House in Stockholm, when they found themselves seated side-by-side at a performance of *The Flying Dutchman;* and talking together in the interval, they had discovered that they had similar ambitions.

Social life in most European capitals could be very pleasant at that time, and these girls had been born into a privileged world. Emilie Louise Augusta Lind-af-Hageby, then twenty-one, was the daughter of a judge, and granddaughter of a Court Chamberlain; Liesa Katrina Schartau was an orphan, whose father had been a staff-officer. Both were good-looking – Louise might fairly have been called beautiful – and both had received an excellent education and spoke several languages. The social pattern of the day might have been drawn expressly for their pleasure; and when they found, in the intervals of *The Flying Dutchman*, that they had serious, if still-vague aspirations to improve a world which, in their own sphere, was already so well-appointed, it at once inclined them to be friends.

In the following summer, 1900, they decided to visit Paris together. This was an obvious choice, because the birth of the century was being celebrated there by the spectacular Exhibition. Faith in the *rôle* of France as the world's chief civilizing power was not confined to Frenchmen, and there was much more than the Exhibition to attract to Paris two young women who were anxious to improve their minds. One of these things was the renown of the Pasteur Institute. Louise and Liesa were both interested in science, and, at that time, seem to have had a simple trust in its beneficence. They had accordingly obtained a letter of introduction to the Institute; and one morning, which was to change their lives, they presented it. Describing this visit many years later, Louise wrote:

'My anti-vivisection life was born in the Pasteur Institute in Paris in the year 1900. Together with my friend and colleague Miss Liesa Schartau I had decided to pay a visit to this famous centre of medical research. We went to learn and admire. The sights that confronted us were startling. We found cages upon cages, vast rooms filled with hundreds of animals that had been inoculated with diseases. They were suffering and dying. The dead lay in some cases with the living. Now and then the young and amiable man who conducted us through the Institute opened the door of a cage, took out the dead body of a rabbit or a guinea-pig, and threw it into a pail under the table. To my astonished inquiry as to whether each animal that had been inoculated was not carefully studied he replied that it was holiday time and that many of the research workers were absent. We saw, in a yard, a wired-in enclosure containing dogs which had had their skulls trepanned and the poison of rabies introduced. One dog, of mixed breed, large and strongly built, who evidently had been somebody's pet, with strangely expressive eyes, stood up and tried to reach me with his front paws. The look of suffering and intense appeal went straight to my heart, and from that moment the fate of vivisected animals became my constant concern.'*

Liesa had shared these feelings. Outside in the street, they exchanged impressions and found they were in complete agreement. Their confidence in modern science – or at least in modern scientists – to improve the world had been severely shaken. Bernard Shaw's then-recent addresses were, of course, unknown to them; but the conclusion they arrived at was much the same as his – that it is impossible to improve human society by means that debase human character. Science may serve or destroy a civilization, but it cannot create one.

Sickened and appalled, they did not form these notions clearly as they stood outside the Pasteur Institute. Words, reasons, arguments, social considerations and ethical debates were all to come. But that morning, a mongrel dog with expressive eyes, trying to reach them through the bars of its cage, had stirred their pity. And in response to that silent appeal, two girls became dedicated to a cause – 'based', as Louise afterwards defined it, 'on that extension of compassion and sympathy without which there would be no civilization'.

They had come to Paris feeling critical of the society into which they had been born, critical of its lack of concern for suffering and injustice; but until then, they had thought of this only in human terms. At the Pasteur Institute, they had been introduced into a hidden world, an epitome of suffering and injustice, devised and created in the name of humanity. And it had become clear to

* Address delivered at Geneva in 1926.

them, in what seemed like a 'privileged moment', that their work lay here. While society remained rooted in this evil, it would be irreformable; it could never attain to happiness and peace. 'The plea of the humanitarian is a plea for widening the range of fellow-feeling.' They had rediscovered, in the eyes of a caged dog, this first principle of the humane movement.

To see a truth is one thing: to share it is another. The girls returned to Sweden, and for the next two years were active in various societies. They studied the literature of vivisection, and came gradually to realize that this was only their apprenticeship. They needed more knowledge, for they found themselves politely dismissed as well-meaning, but ignorant. This style of rejoinder, the courteous snub, had been favoured, perhaps invented, by Lord Lister for dealing with persons too eminent to be insulted. 'While I deeply respect the humane feelings of those who object to this class of enquiry,' he had said, 'I assure them that, if they knew the truth, they would commend and not condemn them.' Lord Lister had Queen Victoria in mind. She was an ardent anti-vivisectionist, and had made her views plain to him. But as she could never find out the truth for herself, it was possible to talk down to her politely. A head with a crown on it is always somewhat in the clouds, and one of the many things that the Queen could not do was to become a student of physiology.

Louise and Liesa were in this respect more fortunate. They had youth and liberty. There was nothing to prevent them from studying medicine. They did not wish to practise it; but without the recognized qualifications in physiology, they could not debate with scientists on equal terms; and they foresaw that this would be necessary for what they now regarded as their life's work. They decided to study in London. Both spoke English fluently – Louise had received part of her education at the Ladies' College, Cheltenham – and in the autumn of 1902 they enrolled at the London School of Medicine for Women. This gave them the right to attend courses in physiology, including demonstrations, at the Imperial Institute, University College, and King's College.

British law does not permit students to experiment on living animals, and their use for acquiring manual skill in surgery is also illegal. Only persons who hold a licence from the Home Office may perform vivisections. The law does not state explicitly that no medical student shall ever be granted a licence, but in practice it is most uncommon. Both students and animals are therefore protected from the barbarity that disfigures medical education in some countries. Professors, if they hold both a licence and a special certificate, may perform lecture-demonstrations that involve vivisection; but in such cases anaesthetics are obligatory, and the animal must be destroyed before it recovers consciousness. Provided that the law is not infringed, therefore, the field of medical education is not one that causes much concern to the humane movement in Great Britain. This is one of the solid advantages of the British Act.

Research, of course, is quite another matter. Virtually anything may be done in the course of research if the appropriate certificate is obtained. Louise and Liesa saw no research in London; but they attended about fifty lectures at which animals were demonstrated on, and about twenty of these were vivisections in the strict sense of the word. Their experience, in short, was confined to the field of medical education as conducted at the beginning of the century under British law.

They were good learners, who were commended by their teachers for intelligence and hard work; and they kept a diary. In the following spring, when they felt they had seen enough, they arranged it for publication under the title of *Eye-Witnesses: Extracts from the Diary of Two Students of Physiology*. This was the first version of *The Shambles of Science*, which, when re-issued under the new title, went into five editions, and may fairly be said to have touched the heart of Edwardian England.

CHAPTER THREE

'The Shambles of Science'

The Shambles of Science has been out of print for half-a-century, but it is still a unique and important book. In its time, it was influential; and nothing that the authors wrote afterwards attracted so much attention. Considering that it was written by two young women, in a language that was foreign to them, and on a subject that is notoriously difficult to present, this was a surprising feat. The success of the book may have been due partly to the fact that it does not deal with research, but only with an aspect of vivisection that is not too harrowing for sensitive people to read about. The whole truth is more than the public is willing to endure. Another virtue was the simplicity of its style, and the omission of technical terms with which the lay-reader is unacquainted. Most valuable of all, perhaps, was its immediacy. There is no hearsay. It is written with the authority of those who have seen.

It does not, of course, follow from this that the authors were always correct in their inferences: on several occasions they infer that an animal was not fully anaesthetized, as the law requires for lecture-demonstrations, and they may have been mistaken. The importance of their book, however, does not lie in such points, but in the fact that it drew attention to the whole issue. It led to a Home Office investigation: this did not change the law, but it sufficiently disturbed the complacency of the professors to ensure its more strict observance. It had also some dramatic consequence that were not intended: among them were the Bayliss *versus* Coleridge libel case, and the disturbances that came to be known as the Brown-Dog riots. These events kept vivisection in the news for several years; and as the book that set them in train has for long been unobtainable, some extracts may be found of interest here. They afford a background, or a prelude, to much that is to come.*

University of London Imperial Institute, 12th February, 1903.

'The tools of the experimental physiologist are many. The simple scalpels, scissors, forceps, pincers, knives, hooks and saws, with their concomitants of cotton wool, sponges, threads of silk, vaseline, etc., which are spread in rows on the glass slabs in front of us, are only some of the cheapest and simplest requisites of the humble artisan in the trade of vivisection. Nor do the various forms of animal-holders, operation-tables, and boards with different kinds of head-holders finish the equipment of even *"un petit vivisectorium"*. Much labour, thought, and study are devoted to the improvement and invention of these, and scores of workmen in the great centres of our Western civilization are employed in the manufacture of apparatus for holding live animals, but all the same, they are only the most elemental necessaries of everybody who nowadays is engaged in experiments upon animals . . .

'The old "masters", if they rose from their graves, and were placed in a modern laboratory well-fitted for new research, might be deemed veritable simpletons because of their ignorance of the complicated apparatus now used . . .

'A white fox terrier has been tied down to the operation-table. It is laid on its left side, and its muzzle is kept closely shut by a piece of string tied round it, and a bar placed behind the canine teeth. There is a wound in the head, about six centimetres in diameter, that is bleeding profusely. The skin and the muscular tissue have been removed, and a hole bored through the skull, and a short metal tube, reaching to the flexible membrane, screwed into the bone.

'There is also a large incision in the neck, and a cannula, at-

---

* Page references here are to the first edition, *Eye-Witnesses*, George Bell & Co., 1903. Subsequent editions under the title of *The Shambles of Science* were published by the society Louise Lind-af-Hageby founded, the Animal Defence and Anti-Vivisection Society, to which I am indebted for permission to quote.

tached to a mercury manometer, has been inserted into the carotid. We are now going to study the circulation in this dog's brain by recording the blood-pressure...

'The strings which hold the dog's legs are loosened, the assistant demonstrator lifts first the hind-legs and then the body several times, whilst the lecturer holds down the animal's head. The lever which indicates changes in the cerebral circulation now records a rise in blood-pressure. This is valuable information, but any person who has picked up a pin from the floor, and any boy who is accomplished in the art of standing on his head knows this without opening dogs' skulls. But to the born vivisector even the familiar experiences of every-day life cannot be credited unless they have been tested by experiments on animals...

'The hour is now consecrated to "stimulation". The veins are stimulated: there is a rise in the vena cava pressure, one vagus is cut, and the effect of stimulation after this studied; then the other vagus is cut, and the result of a new stimulation noticed. Now and then a quite unexpected effect occurs, the demonstrators take it easy, laugh and make the spectators laugh, or reassure us with "it may be due to a clot, or it may be due to a defect in the mechanism".

'When the lecture is over we all go to study the apparatus and the dog closely. It is a fine little terrier with a clean, thick, glossy coat, as white and trimmed as if it had had a bath and good brushing this very morning. There are brown and black spots on the muzzle and the ears. The lecturer wishes to show us clearly the tube in the skull. There is a severe haemorrhage, and he must repeatedly put a sponge into the hole in the head to soak up the blood, before we can see clearly. He then pulls the screw to let us see how securely it is fastened, then unscrews the tube to demonstrate its mechanism, but he is not very careful and drops the screw. It falls into the open wound on the head, is picked up, and after having been inspected it is again screwed in.

'Some of the students exhibit such a keen interest in the experiment that the lecturer decided to start stimulation again.

'We now stand in front of the dog's head. The left eye is squeezed against the table; when we bend down to look closely at the right one there is a look of the utmost agony in it. He opens and shuts that clear, brown eye several times, and never shall we forget the expression. No words could picture so faithfully the horror and the torture which the slaves of a damnable science are made to endure.

'The electrodes are now again applied to the nerves in the opened neck, and with each shock the dog's body shakes and shivers.

'When we left, after an hour and twenty minutes, the dog was still alive. Nobody made any arrangements to disconnect his body from the blood-pressure and electrical apparatus, and probably he would have to be employed for some more "work".' (p. 51)

The purpose of such demonstrations was not, of course, to make a new discovery; it was merely education. Many who have passed through this school have said afterwards that it was unnecessary. But students and former students are not asked for their opinion. It is the professors who decide. And Louise and Liesa found that some of their professors had grown so accustomed to demonstrating on animals that they were scarcely able to lecture when they had to do without one. Occasionally, however, their animals escaped.

University College, February 23rd, 1903

'Fear of death is everywhere: in the king's palace and in the beggar's hut, in the shambles and in the woods.

'But there are some who always hail the touch of death as a blessing – the tortured victims waiting weary hours in the laboratories from which love and light have fled.

'The tormented long for their freedom, but the tormentors fight the merciful death. They are artists in the black art of producing the utmost agony, while the gateways through which death could enter are carefully watched; but sometimes they are not clever enough.

'There is a dark-coloured dog, somewhat resembling the Dalmatian and the bull terrier in shape, on the operation-board. The neck is opened widely in two places, and there are loads to keep the wounds open. He struggles as much as he can till the lecturer injects something into the jugular vein; a peculiar stillness follows. "The animal is now slightly curarised," says the demonstrator. "We want to excite the sympathetic and the vagus end." Another professor is also present and helps to arrange the apparatus; he then sits down among the audience. But the lecturer finds the dog suspicious. He looks at it carefully, and then begins to squeeze the chest of the animal methodically with both hands. Arrangements for artificial respiration have not been made. Was the dose of curare too strong? Many times when sitting near the miserable animals writhing under the scalpels and electrical currents we have wished and prayed that they should die, but never have we so intensely hoped for the deliverer as now...

'The lights are lowered and the galvanometric record is to be studied on a screen. Nerves are stimulated; there is a very small visible effect. Longer and better stimulation; there is a still smaller effect. Stronger stimulation; there is no effect...

'There is no more animal now to experiment upon, so the demonstrator must be content with speaking only.

'When the lecture is over some young medical students rush up to the dog and begin to squeeze its chest repeatedly just as they had seen the demonstrator do. We look at the animal before we leave. The right side of the head is quite flayed; the blood has clotted on the board under his mangled neck. We feel wonderfully calm and happy, but our eyes are wet, and there is something like a prayer in our hearts for the welfare of the little prisoner that has escaped.' (pp. 68–72)

There was an antagonism between the girls and their professors which seems at times like a rift in human nature, a chasm between compassion and intellect. The charge they made in their book was not that of conscious cruelty, but of a kind of blindness.

'"Pain? – there is no pain in our laboratories," they would answer if you asked them, and add: "We have never seen an animal in pain."

'No; it is true, they do not hear and they do not see, for their ears have been stopped and their eyes blinded by the Deity of Selfishness whose servants they are. Pity had fled from their temples long ago, and if she tried to enter again, she could not breathe the stifling air. They have left off sentiment long ago, they do not think of the possibility that animals – nay, animal machines – ever feel pain. And when an animal screams or struggles too much, a faint suggestion that others might mind – because others are ignorant – may enter their brains. But, oh dear, "*We* have never seen an animal in pain" – and we are not going to see it either.' (p. 101)

The sarcasm is unnecessary; because some eminent men, Claude Bernard for one, had noted this want of feeling in themselves and taken credit for it. Inexorably, the professors had been conditioned by their pursuits. The students, however, had had no such conditioning, and they were not completely acquiescent. There was a certain tension, at times, between the demonstrator with the animal on the operation-board and the student audience. Nothing was said. But the girls knew, as they watched the audience, that although they were in a minority, they were not alone.

University College, March 9th, 1903
'When we enter, ten minutes before the lecture is going to begin, there is a tabby cat with neck cut open struggling violently on an operation board put in a corner of the room. Some students

are already there, and among them there are a few exceptionally thoughtful. One looks quite upset when seeing the animal, and turns to the others, saying, "I am sure they have forgotten to give the cat an anaesthetic. Do tell the lecturer." A young man walks out of the room to let him know that they have forgotten to anaesthetize the cat. The lecturer enters, smoking a pipe, looks at the cat, tightens the strings that hold the legs – and walks out again. The humane student, a girl with a delicate and refined face, looks sad and anxious. She tries not to look at the animal, opens a book and pretends to read. She does not like to be called sentimental, and she supposes that it is necessary for science to do these things; but still she cannot help crying when she looks up and sees poor pussy in this state. "Oh, it cannot suffer much," she says with tears in her eyes, "they cannot have done anything to it yet, can they?"

'She then puts her fingers into her ears and tries to think only of the contents of the book. Another lady, who works to obtain honours in physiology, enters the lecture-room. She comes from the laboratories and sits down by the side of the sensitive girl, who at once asks her something which is answered by a laugh. The aspirant to physiological honours must think the other very foolish.

'The cat struggles on its rack as before. There is a small group of women students who have just entered, and who discuss the cruelty in an experiment like this where it is clear to everybody that the animal is not under anaesthesia. Two of them express indignation at what they see, the others make light of it...

'The lecturer begins by telling his audience that he has been working with the cat earlier in the afternoon. The humane girl in front of us starts. He has been repeating Heidenhain's experiment of exciting the sympathetic in order to study the increase in the production of heat in the submaxillary gland, but he has not been able to produce the desired effect. He wishes now to repeat it again to us, to let us also see that there is no effect. He then starts the stimulation, and nobody notices any effect, except the cat, who tries in vain to be spared.

'When the non-effect is satisfactorily demonstrated, the lecturer rings the bell and tells the servant who enters, to take away the cat . . . perhaps he did not feel quite so sure as usual of the sympathies of his audience.

'For how many hours had that cat been stretched on the operation-board, with open wounds and electrodes on quivering nerves, and for how long a time still would it be left in that position?

'During these four demonstrations by this lecturer, nothing has been said indicating that any of the animals have been anaesthetized. We have not seen any anaesthetic or narcotic used, and the condition of these four animals makes it clear to us that they were not under anaesthetic.

'*Once* the lecturer told us that he had injected curare.

'The quiet cat and the quiet dog were allowed to remain till the end of the lecture; the struggling cat and the struggling dog were taken out before the hour was over.' (pp. 117–21)

Already prepared on their operation-boards, the animals were brought in from behind forbidden doors; and when they had served their purpose, they were carried back. The girls did not penetrate the closed sanctuaries of research; but after some fifty demonstrations, they were fairly well grounded in physiology – at least in the physiology of dogs and cats – and could no longer be dismissed as uninformed. In the years that lay ahead, Louise was able to stand on public platforms and debate these matters, skilfully and successfully, with her former teachers. The resolve they had made in Paris was confirmed in London; and a last quotation from their diary, relating to a lecture at the Imperial Institute in February 1903, shows how strong were the convictions that underlay their future work:

'After the lecture we examined the dog closely, and were shown the details of the kidney and clamping apparatus. As we bent down over the quivering frame of the tortured animal, it *growled* repeatedly.

'Who can stand by the side of a helpless creature thus tormented without being filled with a burning indignation against the perpetrators of such deeds? Only he who cares no longer for the things that make life worth living – only he who has lost the sense of shame at cowardice . . .

'We had the satisfaction of speaking to a medical student who expressed disgust at such demonstrations.

'When we left, after an hour and a quarter, the dog was still growling and whining on the operation table.' (pp. 97–98)

Was this accurate reporting?

The law in Great Britain requires that for lecture-demonstrations – but not for research – an animal must be 'under the influence of some anaesthetic of sufficient power to prevent the animal feeling pain'. Louise and Liesa assert several times that this requirement had not been met. On some occasions they may have been wrong, but their honesty has never been impugned. Their book carried conviction as a whole, and it seems unlikely that they were mistaken in every instance.

It is important to emphasize, however, that if these animals did suffer in the lecture-room, the law was being infringed. The professors were guilty of a criminal act. And the immense value of having some law to appeal to, even if it is not scrupulously observed, must never be forgotten. All humanitarians agree that the British Act is in many respects unsatisfactory; but when some go on to say that it is therefore valueless, they cannot be acquainted with the facts, because its value is demonstrable by a comparison with countries where there is no law.

Writing of the same period, Dr Leffingwell gave it as his opinion that more suffering was regularly inflicted on animals in a single medical college in New York than in the whole of the

United Kingdom. He, too, spoke as an eye-witness – one who had far more experience than Louise and Liesa – and he had seen performed, as lecture-demonstrations, some of the most barbarous experiments of the 'old masters'. One of these was Magendie's notorious proof that the muscles of the stomach are not those responsible for the act of vomiting. When Magendie first showed this, early in the nineteenth century, it could have been classed as an experiment; its repetition in the twentieth was an entirely superfluous demonstration; and yet Leffingwell saw it done at a medical college in New York.

'The professor to whom I refer', he writes, 'did not propose to have even Magendie's word accepted as an authority on the subject: the fact should be demonstrated again. So an incision in the abdomen of a dog was made; its stomach was cut out; a pig's bladder containing coloured water was inserted in its place; an emetic was injected into the veins – and vomiting ensued. Long before the conclusion of the experiment the animal became conscious, and its cries of suffering were exceedingly painful to hear. Now, granting that this experiment impressed an abstract scientific fact upon the memories of all who saw it, nevertheless it remains significantly true that the fact thus demonstrated had no conceivable relation to the treatment of disease.'*

Such demonstrations were then not uncommon in America: in Great Britain they would have led to a criminal prosecution. To assert that the British Act is useless, therefore, is either ignorance or obscurantism. It is defective; but millions of animals and thousands of students have been spared by this Act, which owes its existence to the early activities of the anti-vivisection movement; and if the students of today knew the truth, they would certainly acknowledge their debt to these pioneers.

Wherever vivisection has been left entirely at the discretion of

* Albert Leffingwell, op. cit. p. 4.

the professors, in countries where there is no law, there have been abuses which, to those who have not studied the record, surpass belief. Perhaps some teachers have felt the need of an indoctrinated group, and have therefore been impelled to brutalize their students to keep themselves in countenance. How else can one explain the indefinite repetition of Magendie's infamous demonstration? Leffingwell was describing the situation in his native America, but he was careful to point out that it was not unique.

'One of the principle European experimenters today', he wrote, 'is Dr Simon Stricker of Vienna. A European journal recently describes one of his class demonstrations, wherein he destroys the spinal cord of a dog by thrusting a steel probe into the spinal column, producing, we may say, the most atrocious torture it is possible to conceive. The animal evinced its agony by fearful convulsions; but it was permitted to utter no cry that might evoke sympathy, for previous to the demonstration its laryngeal nerves had been cut. No vivisection could be more utterly unjustifiable or more fiendish in its atrocity. And yet with perfect good faith this demonstrator might have repeated the well-known formula, that he was careful to inflict no *unnecessary* pain. "I know," said Herr Stricker, on one occasion, "that this experiment will seem cruel; but it is *necessary* that my hearers should have its effects impressed on their minds." '*

If one of his students had assassinated the professor in the lecture-room, it would have been a meritorious act; and he might have defended himself with a paraphrase of the master's words. 'I know,' he could have pleaded, 'that the assassination of a man who has received so many scientific honours will seem criminal to some people; but it was *necessary* in order to impress on the public mind the atrocities that science daily commits, and to save successive classes of students from being corrupted.' Unfortunately, so far

* Albert Leffingwell, op. cit. pp. 50–51.

from raising a pistol, not one of these young men had the courage to raise his voice; and the silence of the students is hardly less ominous than the perversion of the professors.

They were not silent because they were unmoved. No normal youth could have watched such things without being sickened. In his reminiscences, written when he was an old man, C. G. Jung describes his own medical education in the 1890s at the University of Bale; and he speaks of vivisection as practised there for teaching – he is not discussing research – as 'horrible, barbarous, and above all unnecessary.'* He avoided these lectures; but, like the students in New York and Vienna, he said nothing; and it has been due to this world-wide silence that the disciples of Claude Bernard have been able to conquer the human mind. It has been a barbarous conquest. It has debased our humanity, made a mockery of our spiritual pretentions, and devalued life itself.

Jung saw this evil. 'Horrible, barbarous, and above all unnecessary' are very strong words from a writer who is usually restrained: there is no other outburst so violent in all his works. Then why, at the time, did he not protest? It must have been because he lacked the courage. It takes no courage for an old man, who has long been a world-figure, to be forthright in his reminiscences; but then it is too late. Many others have shared his feelings, and have been afraid.

The Swedish girls stand out from this silent company. It was not for their compassion that they were exceptional, but for their courage. They were prepared to write, to speak, to debate on public platforms, and to bear witness in the law-courts to what they knew to be one of the necessary conditions of a civilized society. Perhaps, at that time, they felt rather than knew it; but nearly all those who have been long concerned with vivisection have come to know it as a social evil; because if it advances human knowledge, it does so at the expense of human character. Power without conscience is the greatest danger that confronts the modern world; and the

* C. G. Jung: *Memories, Dreams, Reflections*, Collins, 1963, p. 104.

progress of ethics is therefore far more important than that of science.

Early in April 1903, Louise and Liesa began to arrange their diary in a publishable form; and towards the middle of the month, they called on the Hon. Stephen Coleridge, at the offices of the National Anti-Vivisection Society, to obtain his advice. They were only slightly acquainted with him at the time, but this April meeting proved to be momentous for them all. Before describing what came of it, however, it is necessary to introduce Coleridge, whose character and policies have left an indelible impression on the anti-vivisection movement.

CHAPTER FOUR

The Hon. Stephen Coleridge

From 1897 to 1936, the Hon. Stephen Coleridge was Honorary Secretary of the National Anti-Vivisection Society, the largest society of its kind in Great Britain. This was an influential position, and he had the ability to take advantage of it. The Society, which previously had been known as the Victoria Street Society, had been founded in 1875; and when Coleridge took up his appointment, only one of the four founders was still living. This was Frances Cobbe, then seventy-five, who presided over its affairs with benevolent autocracy from her home in the Welsh mountains. To her and a number of the older members, it was 'our society'. This feeling was understandable. Frances Cobbe had virtually created it; and it had been she, more than any other individual, who had set in train the events which had led to the Cruelty to Animals Act of 1876 which regulates the practice of vivisection in the United Kingdom. To bring about the repeal of this inadequate law, and to replace it by an abolition law, had become the main purpose of her life; and 'our society' was the instrument by which she hoped to achieve this purpose.

Her possessive feelings were both natural and in character. But when an organization falls under the control of a group of elderly people with rigid minds, however distinguished their past, a time must arrive when renovation is imperative. This can seldom be brought about without bitterness. Those who have set the course for so long are thoroughly convinced that they have the wisdom of age. So they have, but they cannot fail to possess at the same time its disabilities. Age can seldom adapt to change, and is often reluctant to admit its necessity. When Coleridge saw that changes were needed, a clash of some kind with Frances Cobbe was inevitable. They liked and respected one another; both had excellent qualities, but tact was not among them; both were determined, and even wilful. Looking back, one cannot but feel that a modicum of diplomacy could have averted the tragic schism that followed.

By 1897, if not earlier, it had become clear to anyone who could face the facts without flinching that to obtain the complete prohibition of vivisection through a single legislative act was impossible. No parliament would pass such a comprehensive law, and to persist in introducing Bills that were certain to be defeated was futility. On the other hand, no power except the law could protect laboratory animals. The movement was therefore faced with a choice between continuing an ineffectual demand for instant perfection, or planning a gradual approach to its ideal.

Gradualism was not a new policy. It had been first proposed by Lord Shaftesbury in the summer of 1876. In a letter to Frances Cobbe he had pointed out that it was necessary first of all to obtain some law even though imperfect; and that it would then be possible to build on this, by progressive amendments, until it became perfect. Coleridge did not mention Lord Shaftesbury, but this was the policy he wished to revive. Frances Cobbe was opposed to it; and it was put to the vote at a stormy meeting of the executive committee, in February 1898, and passed by a majority. She and some of the older members thereupon resigned; and a few months later, she founded another society, the British Union for the Abolition of Vivisection, to maintain perfectionist principles. After her death, the leadership of the British Union passed to Dr Walter Robert Hadwen. Coleridge and Hadwen, both strong characters, thus came to personify the gradualists and the perfectionists – the two sides of the great schism.

The policy of gradualism was explained to members of the National Society in its journal, then known as *The Zoophilist*, in

June 1898. It has remained unaltered ever since, and this statement is accordingly a landmark in the movement's history:

> *In consequence of the misapprehensions of the new policy which had obtained in some quarters, your Committee deemed it desirable to issue a manifesto defining the present position and objects of the Society* ...
>
> *The continual increase of vivisection that has marked the last twenty years during which the labours of the Society have been confined to demanding its total abolition, seemed to call for the adoption of less exclusive efforts.*
>
> *The policy has therefore been initiated, and vigorously will be pursued, of enlarging the Society's activities and of attacking scientific torture in all its forms by every means in our power.*
>
> *In the adoption of this policy the demand for total abolition is not withdrawn, and no principle hitherto enforced will be abandoned.*
>
> *An alteration in tactics only will take place, and the ultimate object in view will remain sacred and unchanged.*
>
> *Nothing can be done to save animals from torture but by the agency of Parliament, and it is the urgent advice of an overwhelming majority of the friends of the Cause in Parliament that a change of tactics has been adopted.*
>
> *To disregard such advice would be foolish; to continue employing the forces of the Society in a manner at variance with such advice would be a waste of its resources, and a betrayal of the true interest of the animals.*
>
> *We shall go forward on our path* ... *confident that step by step we shall reach that consummation of our hopes which can in no other way be achieved.*
>
> STEPHEN COLERIDGE

This was a reasonable policy, idealistic in its aim and realistic in its method, and it is difficult to understand the ferocity with which it was opposed. The first consequence of its adoption, however, was the resignation of Frances Cobbe; and this left Stephen Coleridge as the most influential member of the National Society, and effectively its guiding mind.

His father had been one of the Society's vice-presidents, and Stephen had not been converted to, but born into the cause. When he took up his appointment in 1897, he felt that he had inherited a sacred trust. He was then forty-three – a man of natural ability, whose family connections had brought him into contact with many influential people. He was the great-great-nephew of the poet, his grandfather had been a judge, his father was Lord Chief Justice of England, one of his brothers was a judge, and he himself was a barrister. All of them were gifted; Bishop Copleston had once proposed dividing the human race into men, women, and Coleridges; and whether this was said in appreciation or in malice, it is at least evidence of some exceptional endowment.

They were a Devonshire family, with a country seat at Ottery-St-Mary and a London house in Sussex Square. The Lord Chief Justice lived mainly in London, and a steady stream of interesting guests passed through his home there. He was fond of entertaining, and he was a famous *raconteur*. It is said of him that during a weekend at Oxford, as guest of the Master of Balliol, he told anecdotes throughout dinner on Saturday night, breakfast, luncheon and dinner on Sunday, and in the train from Oxford to London on Monday morning, without once repeating himself or failing for a moment to entertain his listeners.

Stephen was particularly close to his father, having been his private secretary for eight years, and in this circle he had met almost everyone who was conventionally eminent. Cardinals Manning and Newman, both anti-vivisectionists, were fairly frequent visitors at Sussex Square; so also were successive Archbishops of Canterbury. In his book *Memories*, Stephen has drawn an amusing contrast between the cardinals, who were both emaciated and ascetic – when Manning came to dinner he seldom ate anything but a few crumbs of bread – and the Anglican archbishops, who were robust and athletic. He had tramped Dartmoor with Archbishop Temple, in the days when he was Bishop of Exeter, and recalls that he preferred to vault a gate rather than open it, his eyeglass flying in one direction and his apron in another. To picture either of the cardinals vaulting a five-barred gate would be almost sacrilegious. Still less would they have followed the example of Archbishop Benson, who cut a fine figure on horseback, and whom Stephen often encountered in Rotten Row where both were regular riders.

Gladstone and Tennyson also dined occasionally at Sussex Square. These parties were not pompous, and were noted for the quality of the conversation, but they did not include the fashionable bohemians. Lord Coleridge's taste was for the established and the substantial; he himself was entertaining, sometimes brilliant, but never frivolous. Stephen was not frivolous either; but he was attracted to the aesthetes, the theatre, and the arts. He was a close friend of Oscar Wilde – a sincere one, who did not drift away in the days of adversity. And he seldom missed Irving's first nights at the Lyceum and the parties behind the scenes which followed.

It may have been due to Coleridge that Irving joined the anti-vivisection movement, or it may have been due to Fussy. Fussy was Irving's fox terrier, his close companion for many years, and people have often become anti-vivisectionists to keep faith with their dogs. According to one of Coleridge's stories, Fussy nearly came to an unhappy end. He set out with Irving on his second American tour and travelled with him in the train from London to Southampton, but on the steamer he was lost. He must have run down the gangway to look for his master on the quay, and the ship had sailed before it was discovered he was not on board. But this was not the last of Fussy. On the following night, at the time when Irving was accustomed to arrive at the Lyceum, he was found whimpering and scratching at his dressing-room door. How he made the journey from Southampton to London remained a mystery.

Through his personal qualities and many friendships, Coleridge brought great assets to the anti-vivisection movement. He brought it also a sense of self-dedication. 'As four generations of my family before me have earnestly supported the humane cause,' he said in his evidence to the Royal Commission in 1907, 'my convictions have come down to me as a consecrated inheritance.'

Against these sources of strength there must be set, however, some of weakness. Coleridge could plead a cause as a barrister, but he could not negotiate it as a diplomat; he was often needlessly combative; and he had no sympathy with science, in fact he seems to have disliked it. In a leader, this last must be accounted a defect. It is not by the enemies of science that the anti-vivisection movement will be best advanced, but by those who appreciate its characteristic satisfactions; for they will have the strongest reasons, apart from humaneness, for wishing to see the stain of cruelty removed. Some will be more sensitive to the honour of science, some to the pleasure of its pursuit, and some to the quality of its contribution to society; but all who are in any way concerned with it must be disturbed at this reproach. It is a pity that Coleridge had none of these incentives; but he laid the charge of cruelty unforgettably when he said that the cause he served represented 'the consensus of opinion of almost all the greatest names in English thought'.

*　*　*

On the fourteenth of April 1903, Louise and Liesa called on Coleridge at the Society's headquarters in Victoria Street. They had met once before, but were not well-acquainted. Their book was still in manuscript; but they disclosed and discussed with him the substance of the first chapter. This chapter appears in *Eye-Witnesses;* but when the book was reissued as *The Shambles of Science*, it was left out – or rather it was replaced by one that gives a fuller account of the Brown Dog.

The discarded chapter, in which the Brown Dog is mentioned

for the first time, was headed *Fun;* and its original purpose was to show that vivisection-demonstrations were sometimes treated rather as entertainment than as a grim necessity. The dog itself was not specially emphasized; but the girls happened to notice – and to repeat to Coleridge – that it had a recent abdominal wound. This was quite unconnected with the subject of the lecture, for which an opening had been made in the front of the neck. They also observed that the dog struggled, that it did not seem to be properly anaesthetized, and that it was still alive when taken from the lecture-room.

This might not have appeared legally-significant to them, unless they had studied the British Act with care; but when Coleridge heard their account and read their notes, he saw at once that if the details were correct, there had been two infringements of the law. First, because an animal may not be used for more than one experiment; and second, because at lecture-demonstrations, which require a special certificate, anaesthesia throughout is obligatory. The law had therefore been broken twice.

One of the many defects of this particular law, however, is its apparent hypocrisy: it provides for prosecutions, but matters are so arranged that they are almost impossible. The charge has to be made within six months of the alleged offence, and it is seldom feasible to obtain the evidence within this time on account of the secrecy in which vivisection is usually carried out. Furthermore, even if someone has obtained the evidence, he still cannot prosecute without the consent of the Home Secretary, and it would seem to be a permanent policy that this shall not be given. In practice, therefore, whatever a licensee may do, it is not likely that he will be taken to court; and so it is small wonder that the public is periodically informed, by those who benefit from it, that 'the Act is working well'.

One loophole, however, remains. Anyone who has the evidence can make a public accusation. This is what Coleridge did. Having discovered the name of the lecturer, Dr Bayliss, he accused him publicly of having broken the law. This was, of course, a deliberate ploy to bring the matter to court; for not to have sued Coleridge for libel under the circumstances would have been as good as admitting the charge. Bayliss had virtually no choice. The case was heard in November, it took four days, and was fully reported in the press. Although Coleridge lost, this was probably the best piece of publicity that the National Anti-Vivisection Society has ever had; and the Brown Dog, for the first but not for the last time, was the subject of headlines and leading-articles.

It was admitted in court that the dog had been used for two experiments. A first operation had been performed by Professor Starling in December; and the dog had then been kept in a cage for two months, causing disturbance, according to some accounts, by its howls and whines. In February, on the day of the lecture, Starling had performed a second operation in order to study the consequences of the first. His experiment was then complete; and by law, he ought to have destroyed the dog forthwith. Instead of doing so, he passed it over to Dr Bayliss, who performed a third operation, quite unconnected with the others, and prepared it for his lecture-demonstration. It was then returned to the laboratory, and given to an unlicensed research student, interested in the first experiment, by whom it was eventually killed.

Since it was an obvious fact that Starling had not killed the dog when his experiment was finished, as he was legally obliged to do, he had not complained of being libelled. The legality of his contention that handing it over to Dr Bayliss was a permissible method of destroying it was not, therefore, tested in court. The case turned entirely on the question of whether the dog had been properly anaesthetized during the lecture-demonstration. If it had not been, then Bayliss was guilty of a criminal act. It was this that made the accusation such a serious matter. The onus of proof lay on Coleridge.

Could he prove it?

His chief witnesses were, of course, Louise and Liesa. They

testified that they were the first students to arrive for the lecture, and that they saw the dog in the passage, prepared for the demonstration. Bayliss and an attendant had then taken it into the lecture-room and they followed. For about two minutes, they had been left alone with the dog, and had examined it carefully. They noticed the scars of a previous operation. There was an incision in the neck, in which two tubes had been placed. There was no smell of anaesthetic. The dog was making what they judged to be purposeful movements – arching its back and jerking its legs; and they believed it to be conscious. Witnesses for the other side stated that the movements were only twitching, due to an attack of distemper, and that the dog was not conscious. On the technical question of what anaesthetics had been employed and of how they had been administered, both sides were able to call 'expert' medical witnesses – who flatly contradicted one another.

The evidence was considered inconclusive; and as the burden of proof lay on the defendant, the jury found for Bayliss and awarded him £2,000 damages. This looked like a thorough defeat, but it was not the end of the affair. Public interest had been aroused, and press opinion was divided. Several newspapers discussed the trial in their editorials: among them were *The Times* and *The Daily News*, the one upholding and the other criticizing the verdict. In an article which, as a graceful tribute to Coleridge, was headed

> He liveth best who loveth best
> All things both great and small

The Daily News summarized the court proceedings and added this comment:

'In such a conflict of evidence, who shall decide? We can only say that the whole admitted details of the operation – the laughter of the students, the throwing down of the unhappy animal after the operation, the careless indifference of all concerned – throw no favourable light on the state of mind and morals produced by scientific study under modern conditions. But the really serious issue was evaded by the verdict. It was admitted by the plaintiff that the dog had been vivisected twice before – by Professor Starling. Its pancreas had been removed at the first operation, and the effects examined at the second. But here is a third operation by Dr Bayliss to illustrate the secretion in the gland. What are we to think of thus subjecting a dog three times to the vivisector's knife?

'Let us grant for the moment that man has the right to make use of animals for experimentation in the means of alleviating human suffering and saving human life. But surely there must be some limit to this right. Has it not been reached in such a case as this? Here is an animal which worships and trusts mankind with an unreasoning fidelity. The dog may almost be said to have surrendered himself into our safe keeping. Does not this overwhelming trust – this absolute confidence that glistens in the dog's eye – lay upon us some obligation?

'Is it not worth considering whether the human race may not pay too heavy a penalty for knowledge acquired in this manner? Are we to leave out of count altogether the hardening of heart and searing of sensitive feeling that must be produced by the constant spectacle of such unmerited suffering? Let us suppose that the Swedish ladies were wrong, and that this dog was anaesthetized. But a correspondent points out that the certificate possessed by Dr Bayliss is not the only certificate allowed by law. There are other physiologists who are permitted to perform such operations as these on conscious animals, and no one who alleged that the animals were conscious would be saying anything libellous ... This is not a matter which can be allowed to rest here. We are all responsible for this hideous defiance of the laws of humanity.' *November 19, 1903.*

This was a great encouragement to Coleridge, but it has a wider significance than that. It is safe to say that an editorial expressing such feelings would not appear today in any national newspaper. There is not one that would now champion a dog against a professor, or uphold the claims of mercy against those of science. We have been 'brain-washed', our feelings blunted, and our consciences blinded by incessant propaganda for animal-experiment; and a half-mesmerized press, which is ready to gloat over the latest exploit in stunt-surgery, will not print a sentence on the sufferings of the thousands of dogs, apes, monkeys and other animals that are being mutilated every day. We no longer attempt to justify these things: we ignore them.

In 1903, on the other hand, *The Daily News* was not exceptional. It went on to open a public fund for the defendant; and the response was so generous that when the costs and damages had been paid, the National Anti-Vivisection Society was left with a surplus of several hundred pounds. Coleridge had lost his case in court, but not with the public.

CHAPTER FIVE

The Brown-Dog Riots

In the minds of some, however, the verdict rankled; and the Brown Dog was not forgotten. At this time there was an Anti-Vivisection Hospital at Battersea, which was much appreciated there, and the Borough Council agreed to erect a memorial to the Brown Dog in Latchmere Recreation Ground. The money was raised by public subscription, and the monument was unveiled by the Mayor of Battersea in September, 1906.

For about a year, the memorial attracted no special notice; but in the autumn of 1907, some medical students from University College decided to smash it up. They did not succeed in doing so, and ten of them were arrested and fined. This was interpreted as legal tyranny, and an effigy of the magistrate was thrown into the Thames. After that, for the next three years, the Brown Dog was frequently in the news.

Part of the story has been told by Edward Ford, in *The Brown Dog and his Memorial.** Walking along the Strand one winter evening, Ford found himself caught up in a rowdy demonstration. A stuffed animal was thrust into his face; and when he had extracted himself from the mob, he asked a grinning policeman what it meant.

'It's only them Brown-Doggers, sir,' the constable replied in a tone of amusement.

Ford had been out of the country for some years; this was the first he had heard of the affair; and when the policeman had explained, he felt curious to see the memorial that had aroused these emotions. He took a bus to Battersea; and on alighting, he

* St Clement's Press, 1908.

enquired of a bright-looking urchin if he knew where the monument was. The lad's eyes glinted.

'Our dorg, sir? I should think I know! I helped to fight the stoodents. And if they're coming again, we'll give 'em what for!'

He had found an enthusiastic guide, who led him eagerly to the spot. "Ere 'e is!' What he saw was a drinking-fountain, surmounted by a life-size, bronze dog, and guarded by two policemen. The dog had a mild expression, and wore no martyr's crown; but a chat with the policeman made it clear that he presided over a battle-field, where periodic encounters were taking place between some young gentlemen from University College, the less privileged youth of Battersea, and the Metropolitan Police.

The protection of public monuments is a responsibility of the police, and the guarding of this one had become a heavy expense. The constables took it in good part, but the accountants did not; and they had requested the Borough Council either to remove the monument or to defray the cost. Supported by the rate-payers, the Council had refused. They were determined to keep 'our dorg', and they insisted that it was the duty of the police to look after it. The actual combatants were finding the situation more and more exhilarating. The battle was no longer between learned counsel in the law-courts: it now included a lively element of class-warfare, and was being waged with fists and crowbars.

The primary cause of ill feeling had been not so much the fountain and the statue as the inscription on the plinth:

In Memory of the Brown Terrier
Dog done to Death in the Laboratories
of University College in February
1903, after having endured Vivisection
extending over more than two months
and having been handed from
one Vivisector to Another

*till Death came to his Release.
Also in Memory of the 232 dogs Vivisected at the
same place during the year 1902. Men and women of
England, how long shall these things be?*

Had it not been for the mention of University College, the memorial would still be there; but this specific reference was provocative. Perhaps it was meant to be; but if so, that was not the intention of the authors of *The Shambles of Science*. They did not wish to attack any particular university, but to remove a stain of dishonour that was spreading to them all. No one, however, was much concerned about these questions when, on the tenth of December, the next pitched battle took place.

It began with a meeting of medical students in Trafalgar Square. Such gatherings require permission from the Commissioner of Police; and as this had not been asked for, it was dispersed after a few scuffles. The second phase opened at dusk, when about a hundred demonstrators converged on Battersea for a planned assault. The citizens were waiting for them; and although only two constables were visible to the scouts who were sent ahead to reconnoitre the position, there was a large body in ambush.

'At Battersea,' wrote *The Standard* on the following morning, 'the demonstrators met with a warm reception. Hostile crowds sided with the police, and attacked anybody whom they imagined to be students. None of the demonstrators was able to approach the statue, but at times it looked as if the disturbance might assume a dangerous character.' In repeated encounters between five o'clock and midnight a good deal of violence was used on both sides. But the police behaved with restraint; and finally, the rioters were pushed back into Battersea Park Road and dispersed by a mounted force.

Thwarted in their efforts to wreck the Dog, the young medicos relieved their feelings by breaking up anti-vivisection meetings; and here they were usually successful in creating commotion and uproar. Addresses of eloquence and wit, like those of Bernard Shaw, became impossible; and many speakers were unable to face the pandemonium. On the other hand, tempestuous gatherings were always reported in the press, while the quiet ones were not; and the police-court proceedings on the following morning often made better propaganda than Shavian speeches.

Leading articles in the London newspapers mainly supported the Dog, and *The Star* wrote:

'We thank the students who yesterday organized another magnificent advertisement of the Brown Dog and the cause which it represents. They are doing more for the anti-vivisection movement than all the anti-vivisectionists have ever done, for they are making people think and talk about the hidden cruelties which are perpetrated in the name of scientific research.

'What excites the curiosity of the public most keenly is this problem: at what stage in his evolution does the medical hooligan become the humane scientist? The men who carried mocking effigies of the Brown Dog through London yesterday are the vivisectors of tomorrow.'

Such editorials made good propaganda, but the public meetings became more riotous than before. Louise could meet this challenge magnificently. The girls continued in active partnership; but Liesa, with a more gentle disposition, did not have the combative qualities that are needed by a speaker under attack. Louise had them abundantly. She had been the dominant partner from the beginning; and as their projects developed, she appeared as the leading mind. This may not always have been so in reality: an influence that is unobtrusive is not so easy to assess, and their work was a joint-achievement which neither could have done alone.

It was Louise, however, who drew the limelight. After her appearance in the witness-box, and the publication of *The Shambles of Science*, she was a personality in London. At first she spoke and debated for various societies by invitation; but in the autumn of 1906, at the time when the Brown-Dog memorial was unveiled, she formed a committee to give a more independent character to her work. The committee eventually became a council; and in July 1909, this was transformed into a society that is still in existence, the Animal Defence and Anti-Vivisection Society, which had its first offices in Piccadilly.

The time of the Brown-Dog riots thus coincides with the most active and creative period of her life. She was one of the diminished band of speakers whom no hooligans could silence. A cartoon in *The Daily Graphic* shows her on the platform facing the uproar, elegantly dressed, and wearing, in compliance with Edwardian fashion, an enormous hat. In those days, she was very good looking; and when the young demonstrators were not releasing stink-bombs or shaking rattles, they were blowing her kisses. For those with stamina, the proceedings could be fun; but her response to the kisses was blistering scorn. She was a natural orator, dauntless under attack. When it was possible to be heard at all, she could give much better than she got; and her sarcasms were telling. Who, she would taunt them, would respect such ruffians when they had taken their degrees, put up their brass plates, and assumed their bedside manners? These shafts drew blood, and there would be a lull in the hullabaloo.

On the question of the monument itself, public opinion was divided. *The Morning Post* considered the inscription an insult to the University; and, to redress the balance, published an insulting article on the anti-vivisection movement. *The Daily News*, which had taken the cause to its heart ever since the Brown-Dog trial, expressed the opposite view:

'Opponents as we are of vivisection, we could wish for nothing better than that the medical students of London should continue the form of propaganda which they have recently adopted. The police-court records exhibit the mind of the demonstrators. Some were drunk; others were delirious under the excitement of using rattles, a toy apparently adapted to their general mental development; others, by their own account, were labouring under scientific enthusiasm.

'Neither pity nor regret nor the faintest sense of responsibility towards the animals enters into their state of mind. These men, remember, will be the professors and researchers of the future. The evidence before the Royal Commission has shown that there is really no independent non-professional check on vivisection in this country. It is the vivisectors themselves who control vivisection. We welcome these demonstrations, because we are sure that they will drive home to many people, who do not realize the character of the professional sentiment on this subject, the need for fresh legislation, and a totally different system of control.' *December 11, 1907.*

This appeared nearly five years after the experiments at University College; and by that time the affair of the Brown Dog had spread far beyond the operation-board in the lecture-room, beyond the law-courts, the monument and the riots; it had spread to Parliament, and probably to the Cabinet. All this was due to *The Shambles of Science*, in its first version; and although few people now read this book, it is fair to describe it as influential. It touched only the surface of the question; but the fact that the second Royal Commission on Vivisection was in session at the time of the riots was a reminder to everyone that the subject had depths of great importance to ethics and to life.

Meanwhile, the disturbances continued, and their cost was rising. In reply to a parliamentary question, early in 1908, the Home Secretary informed the House that the protection of the monument had entailed, to that date, the equivalent of a day's special service for twenty-seven police inspectors, fifty-five sergeants, and one thousand and eighty-three constables. In addition to this, large numbers of police had been called out

Bernard Shaw in the 1890s

Louise Lind-af-Hageby

occasionally to deal with related disorders in other parts of London; and six constables were on special duty at the memorial itself.

When Ford published his account of these events, also in 1908, it seemed that every attack on the Brown Dog's monument had served only to increase the determination of the citizens of Battersea to defend it. And so he ended his book with the words: 'Everything has been tried . . . and yet the Dog is victorious. He is playing the part which every known martyr, consciously or unconsciously, has enacted – that of drawing humanity above the limits of its ordinary moral perception.'

Sadly, however, one must record the subsequent triumph of the vandals. In the spring of 1910, after years of disorder, a newly-elected Borough Council decreed that the monument should be removed. Secretly, in the dead of night, the fountain was dismantled; and the Brown Dog, so it is said, was handed over to a blacksmith and melted down. This was an economy to the police, and to judge from illustrations London lost nothing of artistic merit. Something of greater value, however, had perished: a spark of the human spirit had been trodden out.

CHAPTER SIX

The Second Royal Commission

In September 1906, a Royal Commission was issued with these terms of reference – 'to inquire into and report upon the practice of subjecting live animals to experiment, whether by vivisection or otherwise; and also to inquire into the law relating to that practice and its administration; and to report whether any, and if so what, changes are desirable.'

The Final Report did not appear until 1912. By that time two of the commissioners, including the chairman, Lord Selby, had died. The Report was not unanimous; and a Reservation Memorandum, signed by three of the eight surviving members, was appended. The majority of five thought that no further legislation was necessary, the minority of three thought that it was. In the upshot, there was no new law, but some changes in the administration of the Act.

This vast Blue Book remains a treasure-house of information, but it would not be practicable to epitomize it here. The scope of experimentation on animals has increased enormously in the last half-century, and its procedures are in many ways different, so that much of this evidence is scarcely relevant now. It would be possible, however, to illustrate from it a point that has already been made – namely, that although the law in Great Britain permits a great deal of suffering, the situation is far worse in countries where there is no law at all. We shall not now revert to this; but pass on to some other matters brought to light by the Commission that are of lasting interest to the humane movement.

One of these is the ever-needed warning that noble intentions do not excuse an insufficient knowledge of the facts. On the whole, the humanitarians presented their case less skilfully – less professionally, one might say—than their oppponents. It is scarcely believable that the Secretary of the Royal Society for the Prevention of Cruelty to Animals admitted, under examination, that he had never read the Act of 1876. To proffer advice to a Royal Commission on the value of an Act that one has not even read is surely an impertinence. Another witness did not know the terms of reference of the Commission itself. And it is small wonder that when the first volume of evidence was published, *The Verulam Review* wrote of these Don Quixotes with dismay:

'We are quite ready to give them praise for their courage and goodwill, and to shed tears, if it would console them, over their misadventurousness. But we would say to them ... if you can't get correct information – if you can't master the conditions of the experiments on which you comment – if you can't find time to read the Act on which you are offering advice – would it not be better to keep to what you *can* do?

'Be it always remembered that the witnesses on the other side are primed to the teeth. It is their own subject. The experiments are their own experiments. They know all the points to be fenced with and the facts to be triumphantly brought to notice ...

'It is only fair that every statement should be questioned, every assertion met with a demand for proof, every exaggeration noted; that the evidence tendered should have to fight for its life. Do not let us encumber ourselves with weapons that we cannot wield, or commit ourselves to opinions that we cannot defend. Everyone cannot be clever, or logical, or learned, or convincing. But everyone can, with a little trouble, be accurate.'*

The first witnesses on behalf of the animals seem to have made a poor impression, and the comments of *The Verulam Review* were doubtless just. 'We appeal to intending witnesses,' it added. 'Learn

* Articles on the Royal Commission on Vivisection, reprinted from *The Verulam Review*, Elliot Stock, 1909, pp. 34 and 66.

from what has already happened!' This is sound advice which can hardly be repeated too often. But in one important respect, these criticisms beg the question. It is possible to be accurate within limits, but it is not possible for an antivivisectionist to know all the facts: vivisections are done in privacy, which no unprivileged person can invade.

All critics of animal-experiment face this disadvantage, and those who appeared before the second Royal Commission were confronted by yet another. Three of the commissioners – Sir William Church, President of the Royal College of Physicians, Sir William Collins, a Fellow of the Royal College of Surgeons, and Walter Gaskell, a Lecturer in Physiology at Cambridge who held a licence for vivisection – were ardent supporters of the practice. It was evident that they could not be impartial; but there might have been no objection to this if the balance had been redressed by the inclusion of even one commissioner with opposite affiliations. There was not even one. Some were relatively sympathetic, but they were no make-weight to those who were hostile. Consequently, the witnesses who opposed vivisection were examined by determined, skilful enemies, while those who favoured it were being questioned by their friends.

This sometimes resulted in comedy. When Miss Woodward, an anti-vivisectionist, strayed from the point, she was promptly and properly reprimanded by the Chairman: 'What is the use of your coming here to tell us what somebody else says?' On the other hand, Sir John Fletcher Moulton was heard in respectful patience when he said: 'I cannot tell you the name of the doctor, because it was not given me, but I heard it long ago, in the early days of research upon tuberculosis, and I believe it to be true. But if it was not actually performed, it would still serve as a typical example of experiment. I have no reason to doubt that this experiment was actually performed, because the man who told me was a most intelligent man, and he told it to me at the time as having been done quite privately, by a doctor whom he knew, in order that the doctor might settle the doubt in his own mind.' (Q. 12722)

The wool-gathering was not all on one side; and if there was ever a doubt in any other mind that a distinguished man of science can get away with more than a humble humanitarian, this should settle it. In one fundamentally important matter, however, the Commission was exemplary: all its proceedings were published verbatim. Anyone who appeared before it could at least be assured that his statement – in his own words and without paraphrase— would be given publicity and permanence. And it is this that makes the Minutes of Evidence – whatever one may think of the Report – an historical record of enduring value.

Fortunately, there were some very effective witnesses for the humane movement. Prominent among them, as one would expect, were Louise Lind-af-Hageby and the Hon. Stephen Coleridge. The most telling evidence that was given by anybody, on either side, was that of Coleridge. It did not result in the amending of the Act, but it did bring about a beneficial change in its administration; and in some respects, his brilliant opening speech is as fresh today as when it was delivered. This is mainly because it deals with an aspect of the subject that is often overlooked. The obvious and familiar charge is cruelty. But what Coleridge exposed was the maladministration, and consequent ineffectuality, of the law by which it was intended that cruelty should be reduced. This is still a living issue, and one that is likely to have its counterpart in every country where such a law is enacted. The situation that Coleridge uncovered, therefore, points a moral that is still important to humane societies everywhere.

However good a law may be on paper, it will be useless if it can be manipulated by those whom it was designed to control; and however many inspectors may be appointed to enforce it, they will be useless if they are yes-men to research. What Coleridge showed was that both these 'ifs' had been fulfilled in Great Britain. And his exposure remains an object-lesson to the rest of the world.

One pillar of the British Act, without which it cannot stand, is the inspectorate. The first Royal Commission, in 1875, had said in its Report: 'Publicity is the antidote of suspicion, and we look to a reasonable superintendence of constituted authority as affording the means of reconciling in the public mind the sentiment of humanity with the desire for scientific knowledge ... The inspectors must be persons of such character and position as to command the confidence of the public.'

The inspectorate, in the form in which it still exists, was established to comply with that recommendation. But when the second Royal Commission was issued, thirty years later, there was no publicity, secrecy had become nearly impenetrable, the inspectors were virtually colleagues of the men they were inspecting, and there were, at that date, fifteen independent anti-vivisection societies in Great Britain to bear witness to public suspicion.

If justice was being done, it was certainly not being seen to be done. Why was this? Why had the brave hopes failed?

To find the answer, one must first consider the mechanics of administration. The Home Secretary is responsible for the administration of this Act; but as most of its technical problems lie outside his knowledge, and as it is almost the last of his many duties to which he is likely to devote his time, in practice, he acts on advice. He is advised by a department of the Home Office; and the officials of this department must of necessity be in continual contact with, and themselves be advised by, the professional bodies concerned. These bodies, of course, are one of the interested parties; and the other party, the experimental animals or the animal-defence societies, have no one to represent them. Accordingly, in the case of this particular law, there are unique opportunities for pulling strings; and if the manipulators are sufficiently adroit, they may even succeed in standing the law on its head – so that an Act, designed to protect the animals, may be so administered as to protect the experimenters from prosecution.

When Coleridge claimed, in his evidence before the Royal Commission, that pressure was being brought to bear on the Home

Office, one of the commissioners, Sir Mackenzie Chalmers, retorted: 'The pressure has not yet been felt.' 'Pardon me,' Coleridge replied, 'I cannot accept that.' This confrontation is the real heart of the matter. Coleridge had been corresponding with the Home office for years; and although these exchanges were courteous, their underlying theme was always the same – that one party was attempting to draw aside, and the other to keep closed, the official curtains. In this polite warfare, Coleridge showed great competence. It was not for nothing that he came of a family distinguished in law. He was a match for any man in Whitehall; and no one, before or since, has been more successful in penetrating its defences.

His appearance before the Royal Commission gave him the opportunity, which he no doubt relished, of disclosing the fruits of this investigation in the most devastating way. His evidence and cross-examination took three days, from the nineteenth to the twenty-first of June 1907. This has been published separately, and makes quite a substantial book. Much of it is still relevant in principle and should not be forgotten. Only part of his opening speech will be quoted here: it has been compared with, and may have been suggested by, Zola's, *J'accuse*!

'I have carefully read the evidence of Mr Byrne on behalf of the Home Office, and as it stands it has, in my opinion, justified to the fullest extent the expressed and published conviction of my Society, that the whole truth about the administration of the Act of 1876 by the Home Office could never be elucidated without cross-examination by counsel properly instructed. We should have preferred to substantiate the charges which it is our duty to make against those officials out of the mouth of Mr Byrne, their representative; but as this is now apparently impossible, I shall endeavour, on behalf of my Society, to prove the indictment we have drawn by unimpeachable evidence.

'I am here to charge the Home Office officials with repudiating the most important duty deputed to them by Parliament, that of protecting animals from unjustifiable suffering.

'I am here to charge the Home Office officials with having constituted themselves the injudicial defenders of the vivisectors from criticism by my Society in the past, and in their evidence tendered before this Commission.

'I am here to charge the Home Office officials with having appointed inspectors who have displayed such bias that they have thought it their duty not to make detective efforts to protect animals from illegal treatment.

'I am here to charge the Home Office officials with having made entirely disingenuous statements in their official utterances, and with having constituted themselves the mere spokesmen of the vivisectors.

'I am here to charge the Home Office officials with suppressing in the Annual Parliamentary Return the names of those who have taken upon themselves the very grave responsibility of signing the certificates exempting licensees wholly or in part from the obligation to employ anaesthesia in their vivisections.

'I am here to charge the Home Office officials with shielding the names of such licensees as they know to have broken the law.

'I am here to charge the Home Office officials with preparing for the Home Secretary evasive and insufficient replies in the House of Commons to plain questions on the administration of the Act.

'I am here to charge the Home Office officials with having placed themselves in improper private confidential relations with a private society composed of supporters of vivisection.

'These manifold charges, which I am prepared fully to substantiate before leaving the Commission, justify, in the opinion of my Society, the imputation, which we do not fear to make that the Act which was intended by Parliament to constitute the Home Secretary the guardian of the vivisected creatures has been so administered that this solemn responsibility has not been impartially fulfilled. So safeguarded are the vivisectors from the possibility of anybody but themselves knowing what happens in the laboratories, that the opportunity for raising the impenetrable veil that covers their doings can never occur but through their own initiative.

'It will be observed that my Society has been forced to the conclusion that, by placing the interests of the animals in the hands of the Home Secretary, the framers of the Act of 1876, unwittingly no doubt, made a fatal mistake. The Home Secretary had practically delegated much of his responsibility to the Home Office officials, who have in turn delegated their responsibility largely to a private association of vivisectors called into existence for the very purpose of representing their own interests ... and a state of things has thereby been created and maintained for years which we invite all impartial people to condemn as little short of a public scandal.' (Q. 10262)

In the six years through which the Commission sat, this must surely have been its most dramatic day. Those commissioners who championed vivisection were stung by the attack. Neither they, nor the Home Office, had anticipated an offensive launched on so wide a front and with such ferocity. Coleridge appeared before them not so much a witness as a warrior; and with his keen mind, legal training, and thorough command of fact, he made a formidable assailant. There were no platitudinous exchanges in the cross-examination that followed. This was warfare. Both sides, moreover, knew that every word they uttered would be published, and that, in a sense, the world was their jury.

As the situation that was being uncovered might be expected to have its counterpart in other countries, the story unfolded in London was followed with interest on the other side of the Atlantic; and after studying all the evidence that had been given up to the end of 1907, Dr Leffingwell made this comment in New York:

'No matter what the Report of the Commission may be, much of the evidence it has elicited will be of value for many years to come ... It has demonstrated the uncertainty of the methods in use for securing to vivisected animals an immunity from anguish. ... It has made plain the entire uselessness of Government inspection of laboratories by inspectors who are wholly in sympathy with the vivisector, and apparently without the slightest interest in those humane purposes and objects which such inspection, it was hoped, would secure. It has proven the secrecy in which vivisection may now be carried on in English laboratories – a privacy which even Members of Parliament have no right to invade. The Royal Commission of 1906–7 may not greatly change matters as far as legislation is concerned, but the contribution it has made to public enlightenment can hardly be gainsaid.'*

To remove the grounds of this criticism, most of which is still valid, would require, among other things, a balanced inspectorate – one in which a balance is struck between the colleagues of the experimenters and the advocates of the animals. This would meet the requirement of the first Royal Commission that it should 'command the confidence of the public'. But every attempt to obtain such a balance has been fought off. Why? There can be only one reason for fanatical insistence on secrecy in anything – that there is something to hide. 'Publicity is the antidote of suspicion.' And where there is no publicity, there will be, and ought to be, suspicion.

The enquiry, as Leffingwell said, contributed to public enlightenment. It did not draw aside the curtains of secrecy; but, like the Brown-Dog trial, it parted them a little. That cruelty should be descried through the chink was not unexpected, but wire-pulling came as a surprise. With a due sense of drama, Coleridge had kept this disclosure for his final thrust:

'I come to my last charge. I am here to charge the Home Office

* Albert Leffingwell, op. cit. pp. 240–41.

officials with having placed themselves in improper confidential relations with a private society composed of supporters of vivisection.'

The society he was speaking of was the Association for the Advancement of Medicine by Research. This body had been the confidential advisors of the Home Office since 1888 – that is to say, for nearly twenty years. It was, therefore, both influential and long-established; but to obtain any information about it proved to be difficult. Before Coleridge appeared before the Royal Commissioners, they had already questioned the Chief Inspector of the Home Office, Mr Byrne, about this association. He had been asked:

'It has no statutory recognition?'

'That is so.'

'Can you tell us the names of its president or officers?'

'Not at the moment.'

'In every case, does the Home Office receive advice in regard to applicants for licences and certificates from that Association?'

'Yes.'

Although the association was not exactly secret, it appeared to shun publicity; and when Coleridge read these evasive answers, it occurred to him that the promoters of vivisection might have found a back entrance to the corridors of power. He decided to enquire. There was no mention of such a body in any work of reference, and so he addressed a letter to: '*The Secretary, The Association for the Advancement of Medicine by Research, London,*' and left it to the Post Office to locate. In his letter, he requested a copy of the Association's last annual report and a list of its members. A reply came a few days later, but it merely stated that it was not possible to comply with his request. No signature was appended, but there was an address – 135 Harley Street.

Coleridge was now more suspicious than ever, and pursued his investigation. He first discovered, to his surprise, that the Association had been formed as long ago as 1882; and then, searching *The British Medical Journal* for that year, he found a letter explaining its purposes, which contained this illuminating passage:

'The working physiologists of the three kingdoms have expressly stated that they do not desire (at least, for the present) to attempt to abolish the Act, of which we are all ashamed, but to secure its being harmlessly administered. To speak with authority to public opinion, and to bring effectual pressure upon officials, needs other means than those which are suited to the arena of controversy...

'At present a good beginning has been made, and with united action, and a wise mixture of zeal with discretion, we are certain of a good continuance. I am, etc.,

A MEMBER OF THE PROVISIONAL COMMITTEE.
April 12th, 1882.'

What the writer felt to be needed was, in fact, an organization having just the character that Coleridge had suspected – one that could 'bring effectual pressure upon officials', and thereby ensure that the law should be 'harmless' to those whom it was designed to restrain and consequently useless to those whom it was intended to protect. Founded with these aims in 1882, the Association for the Advancement of Medicine by Research, by 'a wise mixture of zeal with discretion', had fully achieved them by 1888, when it became exclusive, confidential advisor to the Home Office. It had for long been the burden of Coleridge's complaint that the law was being administered in this way – 'harmlessly' – but until he discovered this conspiracy, he had not understood how it was being done. Now, much puzzling information became coherent: the puppet-players were in Harley Street and the wires reached to Whitehall.

In common with everyone who has fought for this cause, Coleridge had had many disappointments; but the day on which he exhibited this Machiavellian machinery to the Royal Commission was one of triumph. He was able to say with calm assurance, 'A state of things has thereby been created and maintained for years which we invite all impartial people to condemn as little short of a public scandal.' And he made his point. Not even the most biased of the commissioners could openly endorse this manipulation; and their Report, when at long last it was presented, recommended a new advisory body. It may be difficult to assess the practical value of this change; but the value of Coleridge's evidence, as an object-lesson to the anti-vivisection movement in other countries, can hardly be over-estimated.

* * *

The Royal Commission was in session for six years, and it seems unlikely that anyone will ever read all the Minutes of Evidence again; but one person who did so attentively at the time when they were appearing was Bernard Shaw. He did not come before it, but he gave it – and everyone else – the benefit of his views in a more effective way. In the year in which the Commission was issued, 1906, he wrote the preface to *The Doctor's Dilemma*. Perhaps he looked on this as his own contribution to the evidence; but if he had proffered it in the usual manner, it would probably have been forgotten – buried in what he described as 'a mammoth Blue Book'. Shaw preferred to speak directly to the public, foreseeing, no doubt, that while the Blue Book would remain unlooked-at for decades on the library shelves, a day would seldom pass when someone, somewhere, did not take down and enjoy his *Prefaces*.

As this famous disquisition was written before the Minutes had been published, it can be only a coincidence if any of Shaw's remarks reads like a commentary. But it was inevitable, in such a long investigation, that the truthfulness of some of the witnesses should be called in question; and Shaw seems to have anticipated this occasional scepticism in the preface to *The Doctor's Dilemma:*

'It is hardly to be expected,' he wrote, 'that a man who does not hesitate to vivisect for the sake of science will hesitate to lie about it afterwards to protect it from what he deems the ignorant sentimentality of the laity. When the public conscience stirs uneasily and threatens suppression, there is never wanting some doctor of eminent position and high character who will sacrifice himself devotedly to the cause of science by coming forward to assure the public on his honour that all experiments on animals are completely painless; although he must know that the very experiments that first provoked the anti-vivisection movement by their atrocity were experiments to ascertain the physiological effects of the sensation of extreme pain ... Besides, the vivisection may be painless in cases where the experiments are very cruel ... A cobra's bite hurts so little that the creature is almost, legally speaking, a vivisector who inflicts no pain. By giving his victims chloroform before biting them, he could comply with the law completely.

'Here, then, is a pretty deadlock. Public support of vivisection is founded almost wholly on the assurances of the vivisectors that great public benefits may be expected from the practice. Not for a moment do I suggest that such a defence would be valid if it were proved. But when the witnesses begin by alleging that in the cause of science all the customary ethical obligations (which include the obligation to tell the truth) are suspended, what weight can any reasonable person give to their testimony?

'I would rather swear fifty lies than take an animal that had licked my hand in good fellowship and torture it. If I did torture a dog, I should certainly not have the face to turn round and ask how any person dare suspect an honourable man like myself of telling lies. Most sensible and humane people would, I hope, reply flatly that honourable men do not behave dishonourably even to dogs.'

If Shaw had appeared before the Royal Commissioners, his argument on the invalidity of the defence of usefulness would not have convinced them. Several anti-vivisection witnesses, although with less virtuosity, advanced this argument; but when they did so, a gulf of mutual incomprehension seemed to open between them and their examiners. To the members of the Commission, it appeared unreasonable; but to these witnesses, it expressed the logic of their principles. 'Knowledge', they might have added in explanation, 'is not the highest good; and therefore it cannot be legitimate to seek knowledge by any means whatever. A line must be drawn somewhere; and if we are not to dishonour and devalue the human race, cruelty is the point at which it must be drawn.'

CHAPTER SEVEN

Walter Robert Hadwen

During the first third of the century, the Hon. Stephen Coleridge of the National Society and Dr Walter Robert Hadwen of the British Union led and personified the gradualist and the perfectionist parties of the anti-vivisection movement in Great Britain. Although they served the same cause with dedication, they were in a sense opponents, and sharply-contrasted in character. They were of the same age, born in 1854; and they died, still at work, within a few years of one another – Hadwen in Christmas week 1932, and Coleridge on Good Friday 1936. They would be suitable subjects for a study in parallel lives. Both, although in different ways, were gifted men; and both, although one was a southerner and the other a northerner, were of the bone and marrow of the British race.

The Hadwens claimed to be descended from the Vikings. In northern England and southern Scotland the name had been prominent before the Norman Conquest. There is mention of it in the Domesday Book and at the Battle of Agincourt. By the early nineteenth century, however, the Lancastrian Hadwens were not landowners, but had turned to the professions – mainly to law and medicine. Two of Walter's great-uncles had been doctors in Lancaster; and his father, left an orphan, had been educated by these uncles to the same calling. But when the time came for him to assist at surgical operations – it was, of course, before the days of anaesthetics – he had been so horrified by the blood and the screams that he fled from the operating theatre. Unwilling to return home, and perhaps be forced to repeat this experience, he enlisted in the Royal Marines. After some adventurous service abroad, he obtained the post of chemist and dispenser at the Royal Marine Infirmary at Woolwich. It was here that he married and that his three sons were born – Walter, on the third of August 1854.

The Hadwens loved their children, but they showed them no indulgence. They were not harsh parents, but they expected a great deal. The boys were taught to put duty first, and that happiness came from right living, not from the pursuit of pleasure. And it would seem that they found it in that way.

Their first tutor was the chaplain of the Infirmary. Walter was a quick-witted child, and it is said that he could read English and Latin fluently by the age of seven. This may be an exaggeration; but it is evidence of toil, and perhaps of tears. Such demands, however, did not go against the grain of his character; and they did not make him a resentful child or an unhappy man. Severity and love were blended in his upbringing; and in later life he always drove himself hard and imposed a rigid self-discipline, but at the same time he was a man who evoked and responded to love. He had an alarming temper – to the point of brandishing a poker – but its outbursts were brief, and his friends remembered the 'twinkle' in his clear blue eyes.

When he was thirteen, he passed the preliminary examination for entrance to the Pharmaceutical Society, and was then articled to a chemist at Woolwich. In the same year, his father received an appointment at the Royal Berkshire Hospital in Reading, and so the family was broken up. Several of Walter's letters written at this time have been preserved, and they show that his spartan childhood had not lessened his love of home. As the first Christmas holidays drew near, after eight months of separation, he wrote:

'When we glance over the country and see it in a state of poverty and destitution, families separated, homes ruined and noble-hearted men driven from their native land to seek a crust of bread on foreign shores . . . can we but be thankful that we are all allowed to meet once more beneath the homely roof!

'True, it isn't the same old home, and we shall not have the same loving faces to look upon us as we had last year, nor the same loving voices to greet us, still we may in a glass of pure, bright, sparkling water, drink the health of those dear ones far away . . . I *long* to come home, away from all the trials and toils of business . . . I could hardly believe my eyes when I read that I was to have a fortnight's holiday.'*

Pure, bright, sparkling water! He was only fourteen, but he had already made up his mind to be a teetotaller, a vegetarian, and a non-smoker. Once these decisions had been taken on moral grounds, the questions were closed for good and all. Walter believed in clear rules of living, and he detested compromise. It was characteristic of him that even at public banquets, of which he attended many, he could never be tempted by flesh, fish or fowl; aperitif, Port or Havanna. One sees him as the perfect puritan – perfect, because these abstemious habits brought him abiding satisfaction. After visiting a Health Exhibition in London with his wife, many years after these resolutions had been made, he wrote in a letter: 'The vegetarian dinner was simply magnificent. We had three courses; pea soup, haricot-bean cutlets, and fig pudding – for sixpence, including bread!' He was more than true to his principles, he rejoiced in them. Pure, bright, sparkling water, and magnificent haricot-beans! It was the earth for sixpence.

The chaplain who had begun his education had been a Low Churchman, but not quite low enough to suit Walter's temperament. In mid-Victorian England, with his character and upbringing, it was almost inevitable that he should be drawn to fundamental Christianity; and when he encountered this in one of its most exacting forms, the Plymouth Brethren, he knew that

* Beatrice Kidd & M. Edith Richards: *Hadwen of Gloucester*, John Murray 1933, p. 45.

he had found his fold. By his early twenties, he was preaching from their platform every Sunday, and usually on two week-day evenings as well; and as he never relinquished anything to which he was once committed, this became part of the permanent pattern of his life. He was a born speaker, almost a compulsive one; but his religion was not a matter of words. He strove to exemplify it in every action.

This brought him strength and great sway over more vacillating minds; but the belief that there is only one right way of doing anything, and that on most matters of importance God had shown that way to him, tended to narrow his own mind. Once his ideas had been formed, it was almost impossible for him to change them. He knew what was right, and no power but death could prevent him from doing it. This inflexibility, combined with a gift for leadership, had its perils. He came to be surrounded by loving disciples, but he could brook no critic.

'My success in life,' he once wrote, 'has depended entirely on following my own counsels, and on never paying the slightest attention to what anybody else said if their views went contrary to my own.'*

He has certainly given us, here, one of the keys to his character. It would never have occurred to him that it might be a fault to carry self-reliance quite so far. Perhaps it was the cause of his successes, but his life was not wholly successful; and the same intransigence contributed also to his failures. It may even have been the chief obstacle in the path of his greatest aim.

It was said of him, by someone who knew him well, that he was the most modest of men; but he was also one of the proudest. His determination to be completely independent was carried to what seems an unnecessary extreme. His parents were not poor, and they would have been willing to help him while he studied for his pharmaceutical examinations, or even, as he secretly wished, for a

* Op. cit. p. 6.

medical degree; and yet, from the age of thirteen, he would accept nothing from them but his clothes.

He held posts as assistant at pharmacies in Woolwich, London and Reading, and then as manager. By 1878 – he was then only twenty-four – he had married and bought a business of his own. This was at Highbridge in Somerset. It was a sleepy little town, which woke up once a week to the hubbub of market-day; but Walter's imagination worked a miracle on Highbridge – as on the water and the beans – so that it seemed to him an enchanted place where, as he puts it, 'We started on that wonderful adventure on the sea of life of two hearts made one.'

Four children were born at Highbridge, and this brought him into collision with orthodoxy for the first time. He had made up his mind that vaccination was a dangerous error, but in those days vaccination was compulsory. At the birth of each child, therefore, he was summoned and fined. The magistrates were perplexed by such obduracy, and one of them remarked, 'Do you mean to say that you, an educated man, have the impertinence to put your own opinion before that of the whole world?' 'I have,' Walter replied. It cost him fifty pounds in fines. It was not, however, quite true that the whole world disagreed with him; and the law was afterwards changed to concede the right of refusal which he had been at such trouble to assert.

The business prospered, and after ten years he could afford to study medicine. This had been his dream for a long time. His wife, who was herself a doctor's daughter, encouraged it; and his father, now retired, came to help with the pharmacy. So in the autumn of 1888, when he was thirty-four, he entered the Medical School of Bristol University. He took rooms in Bristol, but he returned to Highbridge for a few hours every day to watch over the family and business, and he continued his preaching there on two evenings a week. He was accustomed to living two lives – those of business and evangelism – and he assumed a third without misgivings. With the passing of time, his occupations multiplied, and for some thirty years he was a general practitioner, a Justice of the Peace, a lay preacher as regular as a minister, and president, editor and lecturer of the British Union for the Abolition of Vivisection. Only a man with the constitution of a Viking could have survived so much for so long. And one feels that there must, after all, be something to be said for pure water, fig pudding and beans.

Hadwen finished his medical education in London and Edinburgh; then he sold the business, which had paid for it all, and settled down in Highbridge as one of the best qualified young doctors in England. He had been First Prizeman in Physiology, Operative Surgery, Pathology and Forensic Medicine. He had been Suple Prizeman and double Gold Medalist in Surgery and Medicine. And he had won the Clark Scholarship awarded to the most distinguished medical student of his year. So far, without a penny of assistance from anybody, he had achieved all his ambitions.

One might have thought that a medical education would have changed his views on vaccination, but it had not; and when an epidemic of smallpox broke out in Gloucester in 1896, he became the centre of a vehement, nation-wide controversy. He attributed the epidemic to polluted drinking-water and primitive sanitation, and launched a campaign to improve them. Gloucester did suffer from these defects; and although they may not have been related to the smallpox, they had much to do with the typhoid that had also scourged the city. Incidentally, therefore, Hadwen's agitation did great good to Gloucester; and about a thousand appreciative citizens sent him an invitation to set up practice there. He accepted this; and in the summer of 1896, he bought the house in Brunswick Square in which he was to spend the rest of his life.

The quarrel in the National Anti-Vivisection Society which led to the resignation of Frances Cobbe happened soon after this move. The Society adopted a gradualist policy in February 1898, and she founded the British Union in May. She was then seventy-six, active in mind but not in body, and living in semi-retirement in

Wales. Her pen was ceaselessly at work, but the battles of a controversial movement in lecture-halls and committee-rooms were beyond her. Who was to take her place?

In her view, unfortunately, it had to be someone who would not only fight vivisection, but who could also stand up to Stephen Coleridge. The rift was deep and the feelings bitter. What the movement needed at that time was reconciliation. It needed a statesman who would bring the two sides together, but what Frances Cobbe thought it needed was a crusader who would put the infidels to rout. This was a disastrous misconception.

The smallpox, the polluted drinking-water and the dangerous drains of Gloucester had for a time been national news. Hadwen's name had made the headlines, and Frances Cobbe had followed his part in these events with interest. It had shown him to be a man of public spirit, one who would fight for his principles, and a brilliant polemicist. She knew he was in sympathy with the anti-vivisection movement. What more could she want? On what better shoulders could her mantle fall? She sent a spy to Gloucester. The report was excellent, but she still hesitated.

The reason for her uncertainty was Hadwen's attitude to vaccination. He opposed it fiercely; and she feared that this would antagonize the medical profession and impede the anti-vivisection cause. There were grounds for these misgivings. The movement needs to be awake to the danger of being used as a platform for something else; for whenever this has happened, since nothing except its humanitarian aims can hold all its members together, it has led to dissension. As it turned out, largely inspired by Hadwen, many of its supporters became involved in medical disputes – arguments over germs, immunology and chemotherapy – all of which lie outside its proper scope.

Whether vaccination is effective or not is a scientific question: whether cruelty in the pursuit of knowledge is legitimate or not is a social question. The one is addressed to experts, the other to everybody; and they ought to be kept distinct. The movement is impregnable when it opposes cruelty; but in opposing any particular form of therapeutics, it steps from this rock on to the quicksands of debate. It is then likely furthermore, to seem equivocal on the very issue where it ought to be unqualified; for to compound the scientific with the moral argument is to give the impression that to demolish the one is to invalidate the other. The more eccentric of Hadwen's scientific arguments have been demolished; and in the eyes of some people, this has jeopardized his principles. It must therefore be stressed that there are two separate questions, that of facts and that of values; and that the one must be answered by science and the other by society.

Whatever her misgivings, Frances Cobbe overcame them. At her invitation, Hadwen became treasurer of the British Union, and then, on her death in 1904, its president for nearly thirty years. The new leader was everything that is implied in the phrase 'a man of principle'. He could not be deflected from the course he believed to be right by promises or threats, by gain or loss, by flattery or insult, or even by that severest of temptations to a fine character, appeals to a lesser loyalty. But he had also some failings that his disciples did not see. He could seldom or never submit the beliefs by which his course was set to a second judgment; not even valid arguments could make him change his mind; ideas took hold of him, and imparted to him something of the tragic impetus that Shakespeare has depicted in men who are thus possessed. He was so sure that all things are possible to God, so convinced that he himself was with God, that he could not measure his powers in merely mundane terms. It would have seemed to him faithlessness to assess what was humanely-possible and what was not, because the obstacles would be divinely swept away. Such men become heroes who lead superbly into battle, but not always to victory. Some wars can be won only by attrition; and these require leaders no less fearless and determined, but more fluid in their concepts, more flexible in their tactics, and who are more likely, perhaps, to be Fabians than Vikings.

No one, of course, has yet led the anti-vivisection cause to victory; and so Hadwen participated with many other people in the state of hopes deferred; but he was not, in the broadest sense, a disappointed or an unsuccessful man. On the bleak winter day when he was buried, thousands of mourners lined the streets of Gloucester as the procession passed. He had not accomplished the work on which his heart had been chiefly set; but he had not failed to serve and to be loved in the city where his professional life was spent, and to be remembered there as 'Hadwen of Gloucester'.

Hadwen and Coleridge ought to have been allies; but, to the lasting detriment of the cause to which both were dedicated, they were opposed.

CHAPTER EIGHT

The World Schism

July 1909 is notable in the history of the anti-vivisection movement because two international congresses were held in London in that month. One was organized by Louise Lind-af-Hageby and the society she had recently formed, and the other by the World League against Vivisection. Two such events in quick succession are evidence of vitality; but a single, united congress would have been far preferable, and the fact that it was impossible to arrange one, although a number of the delegates attended both gatherings, makes a pointed comment on the great schism that had split the adherents of the cause into jarring factions.

What had begun twenty-one years earlier in the privacy of the council-chamber at Victoria Street as an argument over tactics had become a bitter public quarrel by which the whole movement was divided. The demon of dissension had been allowed to grow; and in the rivalry, even hostility, between the two international congresses of 1909, the monster came of age.

Louise and many others had been striving to prevent this. They saw it as a disaster, because the cause was being bled to weakness by its self-inflicted wounds; and they saw it as an irrelevance, because in the face of harsh reality, this was an academic dispute. It was fanned by emotions rather than reason, and by emotions of the less creditable sort. The contending parties were agreed on their objective – namely, that experiments causing pain or fear shall be everywhere prohibited by law. The movement was not then, and it is not now, divided into 'abolitionists' and 'regulationists'. All aimed at abolition: the argument was over nothing but tactics, and it needed nothing for its settlement but common sense and courtesy.

Louise had been working for a world-alliance in which these qualities should prevail; because she saw that for as long as its supporters remained in disunity, the cause itself was destined to defeat. The conditions of reconciliation were simply that neither party should denigrate or attempt to brow-beat the other, that both should recognize that there were sincere differences on some tactical questions, but that these ought not to preclude a common effort to reach a common goal. It was in this spirit that she had hoped to convene a single, united, international congress in London in July 1909.

'The field before us is white for the harvest,' she had said. 'The labourers are not too many. There is room for everyone. Strength of principle is not inconsistent with the will to understand the motives of others.'

Her appeal was for a measure of forbearance, and her hope was a world-organization *that would be broad enough and sane enough to include all.* But the perfectionists would have none of it. Throughout the winter, they had been sending out circulars which claimed that Louise and her party were humbugs, who had no real intention of helping the animals; and prospective delegates to her congress had been deluged with false or misleading propaganda. The world schism, in fact, was beginning to look like a religious war – the one true Church combating heresy. And this struck at the essential qualities of a successful movement – comradeship, self-discipline, and mutual charity.

Despite all efforts to prevent it, however, the International Anti-Vivisection and Animal Protection Congress did open at Caxton Hall on the seventh of July. It lacked the hoped-for universality, but it was none the less impressive. Two hundred and fifty societies from thirty countries were represented. This was striking evidence of the work that Louise and Liesa had been doing, not only in London but throughout Europe, in the six years that had passed since the publication of *The Shambles of Science*. Neither of them, unfortunately, wrote an autobiography, and their lives are not well documented for these years; but the mere scale of this international gathering is witness to their great and fruitful toil.

The presidential address was delivered by Sir George Kekewich, who had played a prominent part in the affair of the Brown Dog's memorial. His humanitarian arguments are all familiar, and they need not be recalled here; but his political remarks caused something of a stir.

The anti-vivisection movement has, of course, no party politics; nevertheless, as the realization of its aims depends on the passing of laws, it is always in close contact with politicians. It is in the legislative assemblies of the world that the seal must eventually be set upon its work. During the early days in Great Britain, parliamentary support had come mainly from the Conservative Party and the Act of 1876 was passed under Disraeli's government. But Anna Kingsford had converted Annie Besant; Annie Besant had at one time been near to setting up house with Bernard Shaw; both were prominent Fabians; and between them they had instilled anti-vivisection principles into what was in those days the new Left. It was to the results of this that Sir George alluded in his presidential address; and to quite a number of people, this political passage was startling.

'We must', he declared, 'rouse the people from their lethargy. Our chief hope is not in the idle rich, but in the workers; and there are signs that this hope will be fulfilled. A new party, the Labour Party, has arisen in Parliament; and every member of that party is on our side.' There were forty-one Labour Members of Parliament in 1909; and as none of them contradicted Sir George, presumably they were all anti-vivisectionists. It is hardly surprising, therefore, that the pro-vivisection lobby should have been disturbed. A society for the defence of vivisection had been set up in the previous year. Ostensibly, it was for the defence of 'research'; but as painful experimentation is the only form of research that needs defending, the word was a euphemism for vivisection. The reaction of its Honorary Secretary, Stephen Paget, to Sir George's address was a letter to *The Times* (July 9) in which he said it was now evident that the anti-vivisection movement had lost its hold over educated minds, and had consequently resorted to the infamous expedient of appealing to the masses.

'The appeal', he wrote, 'is being made, as it never was in the early days, neither to reason, nor even to intelligent prejudice, but straight away to passion and to downright class-hatred. We have the very phrase, in the title of a paper read yesterday by a French delegate to Miss Lind-af-Hageby's Congress, *Le besoin de démocratiser nos idées et nos sociétés protectrices*. Therefore, these societies are "rousing the people from their lethargy". They are "educating the masses". They are beginning to hold meetings in Trafalgar Square; and we are now threatened with the first of a series of anti-vivisection processions through the London streets on Saturday afternoons.'

Meetings in Trafalgar Square were nothing new to the movement, but so far they had not been politically subversive. If Stephen Paget was right, their character had radically changed. It is possible, however, that he had failed to notice a paragraph in *The Times* a week earlier (July 3) in which Miss Lind-af-Hageby's revolutionary congress was announced in the following terms:

'At the opening reception, the Duchess of Hamilton is expected to act as hostess for Great Britain; and the other nationalities will be represented by the following hostesses: Countess Stephanie von Wedel (Alsace-Loraine), Lady Abinger (America), Princess Marie Louise of Bourbon, Duchess of Seville (France), the Countess von der Groeben (Germany), the Marchioness of Donegall (Ireland), Lady Paget (Italy), Princess Ghica (Rumania), Baroness Barnekow

(Scandinavia), the Duchess de Frias (Spain), and Princess Karadja (Turkey).'

So much for rousing the masses! Any serious revolutionary who had the class-struggle at heart must have felt even more upset than Stephen Paget at the sight of the entire Parliamentary Labour Party in such unseemly company. But this unanimous support from the new Left raises an intriguing question: If every Labour Member of Parliament was an anti-vivisectionist in 1909, what became of these convictions, and why was nothing done, when the first Labour Government took office? We shall return to this problem later. Meanwhile, it may also appear surprising that the French Chamber of Deputies, in 1909, was even more anti-vivisectionist than the House of Commons. A hundred and seventy-five of its members, who had signed a protest against vivisection, pledged their support to the congress, and were represented in London by their leader, Lucien Millevoye. And what was probably the most important outcome of the whole event was the formation of an international parliamentary committee under the chairmanship of George Greenwood.

The more one reflects on the scope of this congress, the more splendid seems the achievement of the two young women to whose work and vision it was mainly due. It is morally certain that if the First World War had not laid it in ruins, the political machinery that was here set up would have led to better laws. In the nineteen-twenties and thirties, under more difficult conditions, the world-organization was partly restored; but only to be once again shattered in 1939. Louise and Liesa could not rebuild it after the Second World War, and now they are both dead; but they have left a fine example of what dedicated labour can create. A strong international movement is more urgently needed now than ever before; it exists as an 'unconquerable hope'. International congresses are still held; but none in recent years has made anything like the same impact on public men and legislative bodies as the congresses of 1909. And it is inexcusable that while so much of value has been swept away, the 'great schism' still remains, and that even after sixty years and two World Wars, there are some who appear to have 'learnt nothing and forgotten nothing'. One must therefore say again that what the movement needs today is a statesman, a conciliator, who will bring this senseless conflict to an end.

As Stephen Paget had feared, Miss Lind-af-Hageby's congress ended with a banner-carrying procession – there were two hundred banners according to *The Times* – from the Embankment to Hyde Park. And on Sunday the twelfth of July, Archdeacon Wilberforce held a special service at St John's Westminster. He preached on the meaning of Christian love, and on the impossibility of reconciling the ill-treatment of animals with Christian principles. For the most part, such gatherings are soon forgotten, but there is a lasting memorial to this. It is the poem that Ella Wheeler Wilcox wrote for the occasion, beginning with the lines:

> *I am the voice of the voiceless,*
> *Through me the dumb shall speak.*

* * *

The second congress, which was organized by the World League against Vivisection, was no less brilliant than the first. It opened on the nineteenth of July, a week after the other had closed. Many of those who had travelled long distances attended both, and most of the English parliamentarians did so. There were, in fact, in the body of the movement, a large number of people who did not wish to be involved in the dispute between the executive councils, in much the same way as there are now many Christians who are impatient of the quarrels between the Churches.

The second congress is far better documented; because the World League published a full Report, which contains some fascinating photographs of the notable people who attended.

Their names make a long list which it would now be pointless to rehearse. Princess Ludwig von Löwenstein-Wertheim was president, and there were ninety-one vice-presidents. Among these, there was another princess, two duchesses some marquisses and earls with their consorts, the Bishop of Durham, the Archbishop of Seleucia, and forty-four British Members of Parliament. This last group is noteworthy because it contained four future Cabinet Ministers – Ramsay Macdonald, Philip Snowden, Arthur Henderson and J. R. Clynes – the most important members, in fact, of the first Labour Government.

It is evidence of the depth of feeling that this cause has stirred that so many members of the ancient aristocracy of Europe, and the leading representatives of what seemed in those days to be near-revolutionary radicalism, should have banded together and been photographed together in its service. This is something to set to the credit of mankind. But it also points to one of the perennial problems of the anti-vivisection movement – namely, that people who agree on this question may agree on almost nothing else. They are liable to be divided not only by class and politics, but also by religion, philosophy and theories of therapeutics. The one thing that unites all of them is the conviction that cruelty is an evil, and that the humane treatment of the rest of sentient life is an indispensable condition of any acceptable society whatsoever. That is enough. But only if the dangers of discord are understood and circumvented.

This congress differed from the preceding one, theoretically, because it was opposed to a step-by-step advance; and this was assumed to be a settled question. But a policy which, in effect, condemns the movement to be one of words alone can never be settled in a gathering that contains a number of realistic reformers, and this perennial dispute broke out again immediately, and remained a cause of disagreement to the end.

On the first morning, Professor Paul Forster of Dresden read out the rules of the World League. Rule 3 stated that membership was open to all societies and individuals who were prepared to sign a declaration '*in favour of the total abolition of vivisection, and its prohibition by law.*' Dr Hadwen, the leader of the perfectionists who were determined to stamp out gradualism, immediately rose.

'I think,' he said, 'that we should add after the words "*prohibition by law*" the words "*without attempts at compromise of any kind.*" I beg to move that as an amendment.'

The purpose of this amendment was to prevent the advocacy of any interim measures – of any law whatsoever, in fact, that fell short of totality. Looking back over the long history of this movement, noble in its character and its aims, it seems dumbfounding that so many of its supporters should have been mesmerized into the acceptance of this fatal phantasy, and that at nearly all its great gatherings there should have been someone, some man or woman of ardent sincerity, unconsciously prepared to play the part of Eris and to fling this apple of discord among the assembled guests. It happened at this World League Congress in 1909, it happened in the World Coalition in 1968, and it has happened often in the years between. Because of this intransigence, a movement that is impelled by its own self-nature to unite into a world-force has been split into factions; and because of this wrangle, one of the finest reformative efforts of our time has been reduced to ineffectuality.

'No compromise.' Certainly not! It is not a compromise to travel on the only road there is, and to struggle painfully, if need be, each mile of the way. No end is reached by leaving out the steps between. Hadwen, as we know, believed in miracles, and that may be justifiable; but it is a fact that this particular miracle has not occurred.

The rest of that morning was spent in argument over Hadwen's amendment. The delegate from Bucharest rose first. Speaking in French, she expressed agreement with his principles, but begged that each society should be left free to implement them in its own

The Hon. Stephen Coleridge

Harvey Metcalfe

way: '*Je crois qu'on pourrait laisser à chacun le choix de ses moyens, et ne pas imposer aux sociétés une règle unique et absolue.*'

Madame de Silva, the French delegate, Mrs Earle White, representing several American societies, and Professor Quidde of Munich, a Member of the Bavarian Parliament, all supported this point of view.

'Here in England,' said Professor Quidde, 'many societies are ready for abolition and desire such a Bill in Parliament. In Germany things are different. We demand abolition, but we shall be very glad if we can get some measure of restriction first. In Germany, any private person is allowed to make the most horrible vivisections; and we should be very glad if only we could get a law that would place vivisection under public control. That would be a great progress in Germany; and if I came to our Society and said we must decline such a measure, they would ask if I was mad.

'Therefore, if the meaning of the amendment is to exclude all those who think that we must gain our ends step-by-step, I could not consent.

'The chief question is that abolition is our principle: this is necessary, and in this there must be unity in all societies. In doubtful things there should be liberty, and one of the doubtful things is the tactics in different lands at different times. I do not say that the tactics of *step-by-step to abolition* are the right tactics; I only ask for liberty, and if that is not the sense of the rule, I do not accept it. If it means that such tactics are not right, then I beg you to be tolerant towards those who under other conditions have another opinion.

'It is more important that we should be united on a question of principle, and that we should not have divisions amongst us, but follow the same ideal of abolition, perhaps in different ways, but to the same end.'

Despite these pleas and protests, however, the amendment was carried; and all who could not accept it were, in effect, expelled.

Intolerance was written into the rules, and the perpetuation of the schism became an article of faith. Nevertheless, Professor Quidde's two speeches of remonstrance remain among the important documents of the movement's history, because his version of what the rules ought to be is the only one that permits the idealist and the realist to work together. They must do so if the cause is to succeed. It is necessary to affirm an ideal, and it is necessary to take the appropriate steps to reach it. These are the dynamics of all successful reform. If they are complied with, but not otherwise, what is impossible today will be attained tomorrow.

Laws are a matter of politics, and Hadwen had no understanding of political methods. He may have thought them unworthy. So, at times, they are; but the redeeming fact to be set against this is that the law itself is in process of evolution, and that it is constantly striving, although not yet succeeding, to harmonize the conflict of human wills in a concept of ideal justice.

* * *

Many churchmen took part in the congress. The Archbishop of Seleucia and the Bishop of Durham were among its vice-presidents. Several of its speakers were in Holy Orders, and the gathering as a whole was predominantly Christian. But in spite of this, not one of the Churches as a body, either then or since, has ever supported the anti-vivisection cause. Some of them have sided with its opponents. This is a black portent for institutional Christianity. The issue was, and remains, a test of faith; and the failure of the Church to pass this test, or even to recognize it, points to a weakening of its spirituality.

On purely scientific grounds, vivisection, including the vivisection of human beings, can be defended; but on Christian principles, it is indefensible. Christianity is not a department of science: it is a faith. It is a faith that if man walks in love and aligns his will with the divine will, all his real needs, now and for ever, will be met. There is no Church that does not profess this belief, and there are no facts in history better attested than the cruelties of vivisection. Can the belief be compatible with the practice? Can this be an alignment of the will of man with the will of God?

If, as Christianity asserts, the world is a divine creation, it is inconceivable that it can have been so designed that cruelty is necessary to man's welfare. To argue otherwise would destroy the assurance of God's goodness and the foundations of the Christian faith. But if it is not necessary, then cruelty is a sin, and perhaps the furthest of all sins from redemption. This is not a fine-spun argument. On Christian assumptions, it is a truth; but no Church has had the courage to say so. Far from it. In many of the institutions that the Churches manage or support, vivisection is actively pursued; and even Sisters of Mercy have bred dogs for this shameful use.

Seeming expediency has replaced the spiritual standard; and when every allowance has been made for human frailty, this fact remains: if the Church does not even proclaim a spiritual standard, fall short though it must, the reason for its existence has disappeared. It is the function of the Church, in contradistinction to that of science, to bear witness to the workings of the Spirit in the world. If there are no such workings, as science tacitly assumes, then determinism is absolute, free choice is an illusion, and morality an empty word. Because it has this function, the Church claims to be an authority in the sphere of faith and morals; but cruelty is a matter of morals, and if the Church permits it, then it is fair to ask, If these are its morals, what has happened to its faith?

One of the speakers who raised such questions at this congress was Kate Deignton. She was the General Secretary of the World League, and had worked with its founder, Rudolf Bergner.

'It is expected,' she said, 'in every civilized country that Church and State shall stem the tide of sin and crime. Now I would ask, how comes it that vivisection which was once denounced in England by our great Lord Shaftesbury as an abominable sin, is not acknowledged and condemned as such by Church and State?

'I will also call your attention to another fact: what the knowledge of the practice of vivisection has meant in the lives of so many of us. Before we came to know of these abominations, life seemed well worth living; in spite of disappointments and trials, there was still so much to live for and to rejoice in . . . Then came a day when all was beclouded – we had had a glimpse of hell, and with it the consciousness that every man and woman is responsible for this hell and its devilries in our midst. Henceforth there was no more unalloyed joy for us.

'We founded societies that opposed this wickedness, and we gave what help we could . . . We sought for sympathy from pulpit and press in vain . . . Where is our God? we cried, and ceased to wonder at any crime whatever.'

Where is our God? Surely, where a spiritual standard is upheld, God is; and it was splendidly upheld by the churchmen at this congress. Many were present, and several spoke. They were not hostile to science, but they recognized that to acquire knowledge by immoral means is to betray the Christian standard. Insofar as religion is complementary to science, it should seek to ensure that knowledge is dedicated to God; and if it were, we should never need to fear that we might know too much. But knowledge that is acquired by satanic methods – and cruelty is satanic – is only too likely to find diabolical applications; and in that case, we already know too much. If the Church is to be a true complement to science, it must not sacrifice the standard of love to the hope of material advantage.

The Rev. R. D. Munro was one of the speakers who expressed this view.

'If vivisection is not wrong,' he said, 'then nothing is wrong. I do not believe that God intended men to get through torturing sentient animals medical or scientific truth.

'Our Blessed Lord and Master was shown all the kingdoms of the world and the glory of them, and he was offered possession of these kingdoms if he would fall down and worship the devil. I think we should follow his example and say: "I will not be guilty of this abominable sin. I will forego the advantages which you tell me are to be gathered from doing this. It is wrong in itself, and no advantages that you can derive from it can make that wrong thing right".'

Kate Deignton's question received, one might say, Christ's answer in this address. Many other churchmen have spoken as Munro did, but not yet any Church.

The state was also criticized in Kate Deignton's speech; and without the executive power of the state, no declaration of what ought to be done in principle will cause it to be done in fact. The state, as lawgiver, must therefore be persuaded or the humane cause will have failed. Those to whom the law does not extend its protection will always be ill used – either by the unscrupulous or by people who have convinced themselves that the ill use is justified. Slaves, paupers, defenceless women, and the children who once worked in the mills and the mines have all been cruelly treated. No pleas or exhortations saved them from a multitude of brutalities until the parliaments of civilized countries intervened. These abuses have now been ended, not because we are morally better than our ancestors, the proportion of worthy men to scoundrels may even be lower than it was, but because the law forbids them. Today, there are other forms of cruelty that the law does not yet forbid. Laboratory animals and the people at whose hands they suffer have replaced the exploited and exploiters of a former age; and this new infliction of suffering, in every country in the world, is the greatest single stain on modern man.

The congress ended on the twenty-fourth of July with a gathering in Hyde Park, a march to Trafalgar Square, and a mass-meeting in Nelson's monumental shadow. The square was thronged, and the audience overflowed on to the steps of the National Gallery. There were children in the procession, men and women in the prime of life, and many with white hair; there were no party politics and no sex-antagonism; Protestants, Catholics, Theosophists, and Spiritualists stood on the same platform; and the flags of many nations, which a few years later would be battle-torn and carried against each other in man's terrible initiation into scientific warfare, were unfurled together. Police flanked the procession as if they were part of it, there was not a moment of disorder. It was a magnificent realization of the brotherhood of man within the family of life.

CHAPTER NINE

'La Grande Morale'

The anti-vivisection movement has an immense special task from which it ought not to be deflected. It should not allow itself to be used as a platform for something else. And yet, to keep things in perspective, it has to be seen as a part of something greater than itself. This greater question is that of man's whole relationship to the rest of nature.

The impact of our technological civilization on our environment may make the Earth uninhabitable, and some ecologists have begun to say that man's customary attitude to nature is wrong. This is a new thought to science, but not to philosophy. Since the times of Pythagoras and the Indian forest sages, there have always been some thinkers who maintained that our relationship to other living things should be an ethical one. In our own times, this contention has been given new emphasis and new urgency – new emphasis because the discovery of evolution has shown the closeness of our family ties, and new urgency because of the vast and sudden increase in our powers to exploit and to destroy. We were not prepared for this leap in scientific knowledge, and it has led to a perilous situation, because our ethics are half-barbarous and our powers half-divine. Goethe, with the prescience of a poet, apparently sensed this coming danger when, in the lament of the nature-spirits that follows Faust's terrible curse, he shows how the uncontrolled outburst of a demigod could shatter the world:

> *Weh! Weh!*
> *Du hast sie zerstört,*
> *Die schöne Welt,*

Mit mächtiger Faust;
Sie stürzt, sie zerfällt!
Ein Halbgott hat sie zerschlagen!*

So, by the might of a half-god, the beautiful world is destroyed.

It is significant that it was a poet who had this ominous presentiment; and from Goethe's day to this, it has been mainly writers and other artists, people not preoccupied with scientific and doctrinal problems, who have seen most clearly that there is something dangerously wrong with our attitude to life. This is doubtless because it is their business to understand and portray the world through imaginative participation – to see and feel it as a whole. In consequence, they could not fail to be disturbed – even horrified – by the fact that modern 'civilized' man has no morals with respect to nature, and that his present behaviour towards it is accentuated savagery.

To follow this trend of thought and feeling in modern literature would require another book. It can be mentioned only in parentheses here. But it is important to establish its existence, and it deserves a short digression before passing on to the First World War. No one has given a clearer statement of an idea that was forming vaguely in many minds than Victor Hugo.

'It was first of all necessary,' he wrote, 'to civilize man in relation to his fellow men. That task is already well-advanced and makes progress daily. But it is also necessary to civilize man in relation to nature. There, everything remains to be done.'

This was the outcome of a train of reflections on a summer morning in 1843. Hugo was travelling by *diligence* in northern Spain, from Tolosa to Pamplona, and it seemed to him that the three drivers found only one outlet for their united energies – that

* 'Woe! woe! you have shattered it, the beautiful world, with your mighty fist; it reels, it falls, stricken by a half-god!' *Faust*, Part I.

of thrashing, lashing, goading, spurring and otherwise tormenting the eight mules that drew the coach. He describes the men as three 'satans', and the life of the mules as damnation. But why should they endure perpetual punishment? They had done no wrong. They were the victims of wrong. And as he brooded on their ill-treatment, Hugo felt it to be part of an immense crime – man's crime against nature. So began a train of thought that he set down in a letter:

'My friend, if nature watches us at certain times, if she sees the brutal acts we commit without need and as if for pleasure, if she suffers from the evil that men do, how sombre is her countenance, how terrible her silence!

'No one has pursued these questions. Philosophy has concerned itself but little with man beyond man, and has examined only superficially, almost with a smile of disdain, man's relationship with things, and with animals, which in his eyes are merely things. But are there not depths here for the thinker?

'Must one suppose oneself mad because one has the sentiment of universal pity in one's heart? Are there not certain laws of mysterious equity that pertain to the whole sum of things, and that are transgressed by the thoughtless, useless behaviour of man to animals? . . .

'For myself, I believe that pity is a law like justice, and that kindness is a duty like uprightness. That which is weak has the right to the kindness and pity of that which is strong. Animals are weak because they are less intelligent. Let us therefore be kind and compassionate to them.

'In the relations of man with the animals, with the flowers, with all the objects of creation, there is a whole great ethic [*toute une grande morale*] scarcely seen as yet, but which will eventually break through into the light and be the corollary and the complement to human ethics. I admit that there are innumerable exceptions and restrictions, but I am certain that when Jesus said, "Do not do to others what you would not wish them to do to you," in his mind the word "others" was immense; "others" surpassed humanity and embraced the universe.

'The main purpose for which man has been created, his great end, his great function, is to love. God wills that man shall love.'*

This led to the conclusion that has already been quoted: '*Il faut aussi civiliser l'homme du côté de la nature. Là, tout reste à faire.*' When Hugo composed this letter – it is dated August 11, 1843 – he seems not to have heard of the crimes of science. It was many years later, when he became honorary president of the first French antivivisection society, that he wrote the well-known sentence, *La vivisection est un crime*. This was no burst of sentiment, but the logical continuation of his thought. In 1843, however, he was concerned only to state the general question, to insist on the incompleteness of our civilization, and on the necessity of '*une grande morale*'.

Darwin's *Origin of Species* was published in 1859, and this placed the whole subject in a new context. When Wagner, some thirty years after Hugo, began to wrestle with the same problem, he had more information on its background; and he had a clearer philosophy, based on Schopenhauer's argument that universal compassion is the only guarantee of morality, to sustain his feelings. In his open letter to Ernst von Weber, *Against Vivisection*, (1879), and in his essay, *Religion and Art*, published in the following year, he exhibited Darwin's theory – to which he had given an enthusiastic welcome – as the scientific complement to the philosophy of Schopenhauer and the religion of Christ:

'In the spirit of this unbelieving century this knowledge may prove our surest guide to a correct estimate of our relation to the

* Victor Hugo: *Alpes et Pyrénées*, ed. oeuvres complètes, 1910, pp. 377–78.

animals; and perhaps it is on this road alone that we might again arrive at a real religion, as taught to us by the Redeemer and testified by his example, the Religion of true Human Love.'*

Goethe had expressed a premonition, Victor Hugo had stated the problem, and Wagner suggested the outline of an answer – it was a comprehensive answer, scientific, philosophical, religious and aesthetic.

Hugo's travel-notes and Wagner's essays are not the most familiar region of their works, and there is no reason to think that the English writers who became engaged with the same problem knew anything of these precedents. In a letter dated April 10, 1910, Thomas Hardy expresses a view very similar to that of these great forerunners; but he does not appear to have known that, and writes as if it were an original idea:

'Few people seem to perceive fully as yet that the most far-reaching consequence of the establishment of the common origin of all species is ethical; that it logically involved a readjustment of altruistic morals by enlarging as *a necessity of rightness* the application of what has been called "The Golden Rule" beyond the area of mere mankind to that of the whole animal kingdom. Possibly Darwin himself did not perceive it, though he alluded to it. While man was deemed to be a creation apart from all other creations, a secondary or tertiary morality was considered good enough towards the "inferior" races; but no person who reasons nowadays can escape the trying conclusion that this is not maintainable.'†

This was a private letter; and it is hardly possible that Galsworthy could have known of its existence when, three years afterwards, he

---

* English translations of *Against Vivisection* and of *Religion and Art* will be found in Vol. 6 of *Richard Wagner's Prose Works*, translated by W. Ashton Ellis, London, 1897 et seq.

† Florence Emily Hardy: *The Life of Thomas Hardy*, Macmillan, ed. 1962, p. 349, published by kind permission of Macmillan & Co. Ltd, and the estate of Florence Emily Hardy.

wrote a series of open letters to *The Times*. These have been republished in *A Sheaf*. In them – spontaneously, one may suppose – he again announces the theme of the forerunners, and then develops it further:

' "Do unto others as you would they should do unto you", is not only the first principle of Christianity, but the first principle of all social conduct – the essence of that true gentility which is the only saving grace of men and women in all ranks of life. And I am certain that the word "others" cannot any longer be limited to the human creature. Whether or no animals have what are called "rights" is an academic question of no value whatsoever in the consideration of this matter ... Rights or no rights, I care not; the fact remains that by so much as we inflict on sentient creatures unnecessary suffering, by so much we have outraged our own consciences, by so much fallen short of that secret standard of gentleness and generosity, that, believe me, is the one firm guard of our social existence, the one bulwark we have against relapse into savagery. Once admit that we have the right to inflict unnecessary suffering, and you have destroyed the very basis of human society ...

'Nothing so endangers the fineness of the human heart as the possession of power over others; nothing so corrodes it as the callous or cruel exercise of that power; and the more helpless the creature over whom power is cruelly or callously exercised, the more the human heart is corroded. It is recognition of this truth which has brought the conscience of our age, and with it the law, to say that we cannot any longer with impunity regard ourselves as licensed torturers of the rest of creation; that we cannot, for our own sakes, afford it.

'To those who, tempted by the devil of irreflection, say, "But this is the creed of sentiment and softness," I return the answer, "Sirs, no man ever became a stoic, and acquired the virtues of fortitude and courage, by inflicting pain on others." '*

* John Galsworthy: *A Sheaf*, Heinemann, 1916, pp. 59–62.

Neither Hardy nor Galsworthy was a Christian at the time when these letters were written; and it is therefore somewhat remarkable that both should have appealed to the words of Christ, and that official Christianity should have repudiated them.

One is tempted to prolong this 'digression', because many modern writers, probably most, have had similar feelings and insights. There is no space to do so in this book, but one other name cannot be omitted. This is Alfred Russel Wallace, the co-discoverer of Natural Selection. It will be recalled that when Wallace was recovering from a fever at Ternate in the Malay Archipelago early in 1858, this concept came to him in what seemed like a moment of revelation. He at once wrote to Darwin; and when Darwin opened the letter, he found to his amazement that it contained a draft of his own unpublished theory set out almost in his own words. This led to the reading of the famous joint-paper before the Linnean Society on July 1, 1858, and so marked the beginning of one of the greatest revolutions in human thought.

Wallace might have appeared before both the Royal Commissions on vivisection. In fact he did not; but in his last book, published in 1912, he gave his views on the subject. He had a special reason for doing so in this work, because it also sets out his theory of pain. Wallace believed that the perception of pain is most acute in modern European man, less so in primitive races, and that it gradually diminishes in descending the scale of evolution. He was anxious, however, that this theory should not be used as an excuse for callous research, and this led him to comment on the subject.

'The moral argument against vivisection remains whether the animals suffer as much as we do or only half as much. The bad effect on the operator and on the students and spectators remains; the undoubted fact that the practice tends to produce a callousness and a passion for experiment, which leads to unauthorized experiments in hospitals on unprotected patients, remains; the horrible callousness of binding the sufferers in the operating trough, so that they cannot express their pain by sound or motion, remains; their treatment, after the experiment, by careless attendants, brutalized by custom, remains; the argument of the uselessness of a large proportion of the experiments, repeated again and again on scores and hundreds of animals, to confirm or refute the work of other vivisectors, remains; and, finally, the iniquity of its use to demonstrate already-established facts to physiological students in hundreds of colleges and schools all over the world, remains. I myself am thankful to be able to believe that even the highest animals below ourselves do not feel so acutely as we do; but that fact does not in any way remove my fundamental disgust at vivisection as being brutalizing and immoral.'*

It may be that in our own time the word 'immoral' has lost something of its force, in some fields we are less sure of what it ought to mean; but one word that has not and never will lose its meaning is 'disgust'; and when Wallace reviewed the practice of vivisection, disgust was his 'fundamental' feeling.

One cannot simply brush aside the fact that a veritable constellation of creative minds have made the same criticism, the same protest, the same appeal. If our culture may be said to have a voice, it is theirs. But the great institutions of science have paid no attention to it whatever. It may be that a process of conditioning is involved in the collective pursuit of science that closes the mind to any consideration that might appear to conflict with its advance. But that the men who are amassing this body of knowledge should be heedless – even ignorant – of the judgment of those who have created the civilization which it is now in their power to destroy is perilous arrogance; for the sciences, disdainful of the

* Alfred Russell Wallace: *The World of Life*, Chapman & Hall, 2nd ed. 1914, p. 381.

ethics of life, could obliterate in a day the whole human inheritance that the arts have built up over thousands of years.

> *Weh! Weh!*
> *Du hast sie zerstört,*
> *Die schöne Welt!*

CHAPTER TEN

The Science of Death

In the spring of 1914, Dr Hadwen attended a congress in Rome. Acting as interpreter to the party was one of his devoted followers, Ethel Douglas Hume, who has left an account of this journey in her book, *The Mind Changers*. Her most vivid recollection of Rome was of a visit to a research institute. She went there alone on the first occasion, but returned to it with Hadwen:

'Next day, the last in Rome, I took Dr Hadwen over the pathological laboratories, and gained for him a permit to view the physiological laboratory. There was the more urgency for this because my sharp ears had caught a faint, heart-rending wail of a dog in the distance.

'We found the medical director of the second laboratory most polite and affable. He was just the type of man that no one would dream of suspecting of cruelty. He discoursed pleasantly on his work on the pancreas and internal organs . . . Finally we asked to see his experimental animals. He regretted this to be impossible. The attendant was away with the key of the animal-house and would not be back until the afternoon.

'We saw no reason against our return as well as that of the attendant. So, at half-past four o'clock, we climbed the stairs of the big building and crossed a flat roof to an outhouse. Beyond this, purple wistaria showered long, delicate tendrils. Above us, there was no cloud in a vivid blue sky. It was a scene of peace and beauty. The outhouse had a door ajar. Someone tried to pull it to just as we pushed it open. We entered to find the doctor, in a long white operating coat, standing over a trough on which a large dog was being held down on its back by an attendant. Precautions against a bite had been taken, for the unfortunate creature's jaw and neck had cords tightly binding them. His chest was heaving while the vivisector inserted a probe into a fistula, a round opening, which exposed the pancreas. Beneath this gaping wound was a long cut in the abdomen through which the intestines could be seen, highly inflamed and gangrenous.

' "This dog is very ill," the doctor exclaimed, looking up. He was considerably startled by our intrusion.

' "Is he anaesthetized?" I asked.

' "Oh, no; I am only dressing the wound. Besides he is too ill to feel anything."

'I moved round to the animal's head and saw those faithful dog's eyes bright with fever and the extremity of unbearable anguish. They gazed at me in heart-rending entreaty. Just then, his tormentor rubbed iodine on the wounds, and the unhappy creature commenced to moan and whine feebly . . .

'Meanwhile the attendant had grasped the dog by his neck and tail and swung him to the ground . . . What a sight he was, mere skin and bone, with his neck rubbed raw from frantic, vain attempts to reach and lick those terrible openings in his mangled body.

'On the open roof, many more dogs were to be seen. One was a walking skeleton. All looked wretched and underfed. There was one exception, a pretty black pomeranean, which frisked and barked, her sufferings presumably still before her.

'Little sleep did I get that night . . . I was haunted by a demon in a long white coat bending over a vivisection trough on which mangled creatures agonized.'*

Almost by accident, she had penetrated one of the 'sanctuaries' of research – one of many thousands – to which the layman has no access and in the reality of which he would rather not believe. That sleepless night was her last memory of Rome, but the vision

* E. Douglas Hume, *The Mind Changers*, Hume Books Trust, 1939, p. 261.

of the vivisecting-table kept returning on her homeward journey. It was evening, as the train sped across the former battle-fields of the Franco-Prussian War. There will be no end to wars, she thought while we are so uncivilized as to torture the innocent for our supposed advantage. As she sat watching a blood-red setting sun, the blood of the battle-fields and the blood of the laboratories seemed to mingle in her imagination, and the red sky itself became a symbol of man's barbarous conquests. It was April 1914.

* * *

A year later, on April 22, 1915, an immense biomedical experiment was made on man. Preparatory experiments had been made on animals, but this was the crucial test. It took place at Ypres in the late afternoon, and is thus described in a dispatch by Field-Marshal Sir John French:

'Following a heavy bombardment, the enemy attacked the French Division at about 5 p.m., using asphyxiating gases for the first time. Aircraft reported that at about 5 p.m. thick yellow smoke had been seen issuing from the German trenches between Langemarch and Bixschoote. What follows almost defies description. The effects of these poisonous gases was so virulent as to render the whole of the line held by the French Division mentioned above practically incapable of any action at all. It was at first impossible for anyone to realize what had actually happened. The smoke and fumes hid everything from sight, and hundreds of men were thrown into a comatose or dying condition, and within an hour the whole position had to be abandoned, together with about fifty guns.'

The gas used on this occasion was chlorine. There were others to come before 1918, and many more deadly gases have been invented since. But this first attack exerted a fascination on the world that nothing could afterwards equal until the first nuclear bomb fell on

Japan. It was not the casualties that evoked this horrified attention: it was the sudden disclosure to all humanity of the science of death.

The First World War began as one of explosives. When it ended, the guns on both sides were firing more than fifty per cent of gas-filled shells. Today, the intercontinental ballistic missiles, poised in readiness on the launching-pads of the opposing Great Powers, are said to be loaded with an even higher percentage of chemical warheads. Be that as it may, they have the capability of destroying the human race several times over. April 1915 was therefore the beginning of a new era in warfare, and showed that a scientific innovation, suddenly sprung on an unsuspecting adversary, may be more effective than the massing of a million men. The dream of research in this field is not the improvement of an existing weapon, but the development of a revolutionary weapon that will settle hostilities at a single stroke. The chemists almost succeeded in doing this in the First World War, and the nuclear physicists achieved it completely in the second. It is now the biologists who are in the forefront of research, and who may possibly produce the ultimate weapon.

Professor Haber, the distinguished chemist to whose genius the first gas attack was chiefly due, was present on the battle-field at Ypres to watch this great experiment. From the scientific standpoint, it was brilliantly successful. If the acquisition of knowledge could justify everything, it would justify this. As has been said, it began a revolution. Thenceforth, the general staffs, pitting their military skills against each other, would not really be the masterminds in war: behind them there would always be teams of scientists, whose indefatigable researches would open the way to – would compel, in fact – new strategic conceptions.

It was mainly because a chasm still existed between these ways of thought that the scientific success at Ypres did not lead at once to a military victory. This new conception of warfare was not that of a soldier, but of a professor; and the general staff had felt far from at home with it. If they had had more faith in the professors, and had been poised to exploit this initial havoc, they might have broken through to the Channel ports, and perhaps won the war. As such confidence was naturally lacking, the advantages of surprise were lost; and it was not long before scientists on the other side had devised protective and then retaliatory measures. Considered simply as an experiment in destruction, however, the first gas-attack at Ypres was a triumph: it killed five thousand men and inflicted many times that number of casualties.

There were two contrasting reactions to this event. One was a dim recognition that if an ethic cannot be imposed on science while it is still in its childhood, it will, in its maturity, lay the world in ashes; the other, not dim but clear and energetic, was the determination, both on the battle-field and in the laboratory, to out-Herod Herod. While the war lasted, this was inevitable; and it is not surprising that there is a tone of satisfaction in the dispatch which Field-Marshal Sir Douglas Haig, as he then was, wrote on December 23, 1916:

'The employment by the enemy of gas and liquid flame as weapons of offence compelled us not only to discover ways to protect our troops from their effects, but also to devise means to make use of the same instruments of destruction. Great fertility of invention has been shown, and very great credit is due to the special personnel employed for the rapidity and success with which these new arms have been developed and perfected. The army owes its thanks to the chemists, physiologists, and physicists of the highest rank who devoted their energies to enable us to surpass the enemy in the use of a means of warfare which took the civilized world by surprise.'

Chemists and physiologists, experiments and trials. Haig does not mention the animals – not many writers do – but it was, and is, on their mutilated bodies that such deadly researches are carried out. While the war continued, this could hardly have been otherwise. A nation engaged in such a struggle stifles most of its qualms. In any case, these particular qualms had been stifled long ago, and what is notable is the new aim. Previously, it had been argued that any cruelty was permissible if there was a chance of its leading to knowledge that would save or prolong human life: after 1915, it was tacitly conceded that any experiment on animals that might advance the science of human destruction was imperative. In wartime, this was much the stronger argument; but not many people cared to state it plainly. Science does not willingly expose its other face. As we know, all painful experiments are done in privacy; and the secrecy of these new investigations was further protected by barbed wire.

Both the World Wars gave fresh impetus to vivisection. They also weakened the national societies that were fighting it, and twice reduced the international movement to ruins. At the same time, the academies of science and the universities – world-education, that is to say, at its highest level – were shaping a new climate of opinion in which cruelty is accepted and its practitioners honoured. It is a sowing that will reap the whirlwind. But to lay the blame on science would be wrong. It is we who are unworthy of science; and for as long as we acquire knowledge by means that are intrinsically evil, we shall continue to be unfitted for its possession. If we are to wield all-but godlike powers, it is imperative that we should make a corresponding ethical advance. If we fail to do that, then Professor Haber's great experiment exhibits the alternative – the secret hell of our laboratories suddenly extended to ourselves.

CHAPTER ELEVEN

The New Sowers

Some day, the history of the anti-vivisection movement will be written in full; and this will include the story, valiant but sad, of the rebuilding of the international work between the wars, and of its second disruption. There is no space for this long narrative here. Only a few special events and some of the outstanding personalities of the period can be mentioned. Many new workers then entered the field: to select a few names is arbitrary and invidious, and the author hopes to be forgiven for his omissions.

Most of those who were notable in the Edwardian age were still active. Louise Lind-af-Hageby had been joined by the Duchess of Hamilton and Brandon, who became one of the moving spirits in the Animal Defence and Anti-Vivisection Society between the wars. Her tireless work is an example of the universal charity that Christian beliefs always should – but not often do – inspire; and the Ferne Animal Sanctuary in Dorsetshire, which was her creation, remains her lasting memorial. Margaret Ford, who had succeeded Kate Deignton as secretary of the World League, is another who will not be forgotten, because World Day for Animals, which is now widely celebrated on the first Sunday in October, was her conception. The Scottish author Alasdair Alpin MacGregor will be remembered with Ruskin, who resigned his professorship at Oxford when a vivisection laboratory was set up there; because MacGregor made a similar protest to the University of Edinburgh. He has written an account of this in *The Golden Lamp*:

'This foretaste of Paradise came to an end, very definitely and poignantly, with my discovery of something which was to destroy any hope of true happiness I might otherwise have found. The discovery related solely to the practice of experimentation upon living, sentient animals, and the suffering it entails for them – a practice now so universally and so legally established, approved, defended, and recklessly endowed.

'The impact of all this knocked the bottom out of any deep concern I might have entertained hitherto for the supposed well-being of human society. It extinguished in me just that flickering ray of hope for mankind which had survived my spell in the trenches of Flanders, of Artois and Picardy.

'But, if hope had now vanished, conviction had taken its place: I was absolutely and resolutely certain that by no honourable standards could vivisection be justified ... In 1929 I returned my graduation diplomas to the Principal and Vice-Chancellor of Edinburgh University, the late Sir Alfred Ewing, as a protest against my Alma Mater's extensive vivisectional activities. I asked that my name be deleted from the University's records ... My request was granted; and my association with Edinburgh University, except where a few of my professors and contemporaries were concerned, came officially to an end, then and there.'

MacGregor is one of the many people whose lives have been darkened by the cruelty of science: 'So my Happy Day had gone from the shining fields, never to return with anything of its first joyous intensity. That peace at eventide, induced by the glow of my Golden Lamp, had been disrupted for ever.'*

Stephen Coleridge, although in his sixties, was then still at work; and during the war he had published a book, *Vivisection: A Heartless Science*. He could hardly have chosen a more unpropitious time, and his book did not receive the attention it deserved. But

---

* Alasdair Alpin MacGregor: *The Golden Lamp*, Michael Joseph, 1964, pp. 250–52.

from the point of view of the cause for which it was written, if it had done no more than one thing, it would have to be considered an influential work. Soon after it appeared, it was read by a boy of sixteen. It made a deep impression on him, and he thereupon informed his father that he intended to devote his life to this cause.

Coleridge could have felt satisfied with his book, even if it had then sunk into oblivion; but James Metcalfe was far from pleased with this decision of his youngest son. It threatened to interfere with his education, because Harvey was an impetuous boy. *Incipit vita nova*! He wished to embark immediately on the 'new life' which this book had opened to him. There was a vision in his mind, words on his tongue; he wanted only a public and a platform – and he wanted them at once.

It is to be hoped that Harvey Metcalfe, who is now Chairman of the Scottish Society for the Prevention of Vivisection, will write his autobiography. Who else could explain how a boy in his teens, in face of parental disapproval and unconnected with any society, became a public speaker, travelling long distances by invitation, and undaunted by the large audiences that he frequently drew? As a natural psychic sensitive, he would perhaps say that something was 'given' to him on these occasions, and that this astonishing power was not entirely his own. In any case, he was keenly aware that this was not only a social question, it was also a religious and a spiritual one.

Even in those early days, he also found time to begin writing on psychical problems; and in this field he had the good fortune to be encouraged by Sir Arthur Conan Doyle. Conan Doyle was then the most highly-paid author in the world, and it was due to his sponsorship that young Metcalfe first found himself in print. In 1927, on the recommendation of Louise Lind-af-Hageby and the Duchess of Hamilton and Brandon, he joined the staff of the society that he has served ever since, the Scottish Society for the Prevention of Vivisection.

This society had originated in 1902, through the joint efforts of

Miss Netta Ivory and Stephen Coleridge, as the Edinburgh branch of the National Anti-Vivisection Society. In 1911, the branch became independent, under the title of the Scottish Co-operative Anti-Vivisection Society. The name was thought to be awkward and was changed in the following year, but it exactly described the new society's intentions. It desired to work in co-operation with all who were opposing vivisection, and to bring to an end the feuds by which the movement was being torn apart. Its first three presidents were the Earl of Haddington, the Duchess of Hamilton and Brandon, and Miss Lind-af-Hageby; and its fourth, previously its chairman for many years, is Mr A. C. T. Nisbet, whose life has been devoted to the animal-protection cause.

When he joined the society as lecturer and organizer, Harvey Metcalfe's first concern was to increase its membership; and he set about doing so in the hard way – knocking on doors through the length and breadth of Scotland. Many were shut in his face, but many opened, and hundreds of new subscribers were thus secured. He was blessed in this work by the companionship of an ideal helpmate, and if Scotland is better informed on vivisection than most other countries, it is to Mr and Mrs Metcalfe and their devoted fellow workers that this is largely due. For weeks on end, in storm and fine weather, the Metcalfes would travel the country in their caravan, speaking from every kind of platform and knocking on innumerable doors. Few subjects are more difficult to speak on, and few are more unwillingly heard; but today, the influence of the S.S.P.V. has spread far beyond Scotland. This is mainly by reason of its films and beautifully-illustrated Annual Reviews; but Metcalfe estimates that he has travelled more than a million miles on anti-vivisection business. And for him this has been a pilgrimage inspired by a faith.

'If I were able to confer one spiritual talent on the human race,' he wrote, 'I would choose that of simple kindness towards all living creatures; for it is my conviction that this would bring other virtues, many and varied, in its train; and that it would lay the foundation for the Kingdom of God on earth, instead of leaving it to a future life.'

* * *

The anti-vivisection movement is not merely a negative one. It is *against* cruelty, but it is also *for* science without cruelty. It is a 'charity' in the only full sense of the word, for it maintains that charitable ends must be reached by charitable methods. The attempt to attain a good object by inflicting pain on millions of animals can never, at the best, be more than doubtful charity; and knowledge without pity may well be the greatest danger that besets the world. Until the stain of cruelty has been wholly removed from science, it cannot display its essential splendour; and the movement has therefore never failed to have the support of a certain number of scientists. A doctor of medicine, George Hoggan, was one of the four founders of what is now the National Anti-Vivisection Society. The three others were Frances Cobbe, the Earl of Shaftesbury and the Archbishop of York; but it was Dr Hoggan, in a letter written to Frances Cobbe in November 1875, who made the first proposal that a society should be formed.

The institutions of science have condoned its cruelties, but many individual scientists have not; and among the 'new sowers' of the inter-war years, it is pleasing to find a Fellow of the Royal Society. This was George F. C. Searle, Lecturer in Experimental Physics at the University of Cambridge, who wrote the preface to what is probably the most important pamphlet that the Animal Defence and Anti-Vivisection Society has ever published. In his preface, Dr Searle explains how he himself was drawn into the movement, as many others have been, by the direct appeal of the animals themselves.

'I trust that by this Essay,' he wrote, 'the ears of many will be attuned to hear the cries of the animals above the voices of the world, and that they may be driven to realize the horrors of vivisection and be impelled to enquire further into the matter. In my own case, when I heard the cries of dogs on laboratory premises, I was driven to come out uncompromisingly against vivisection. Some might consider this a dangerous step, but no particular harm has come to me in consequence. What happened to me may happen to anyone who allows indisputable fact to influence his actions ...

'He who can read this *Survey* with any care and still believe that vivisection emerges unscathed is in a pitiable state. Probably his intelligence is clouded by his intellect.'

It is an encouragement to find a Fellow of the Royal Society whose intelligence has not been clouded in this subtle manner; and the importance of this pamphlet lies not so much in its arguments, which are familiar, as in the authority with which they were advanced. In addition to Dr Searle, it was signed by forty-six persons – all of whom held degrees in science, and nearly all in medicine; and the document which they compiled and signed was an unequivocal denunciation.

At the outset, they were careful to define what they were against; but this may now require a little more clarification. The word 'vivisection' was not coined by opponents of the practice. It was being used by physiologists early in the eighteenth century – possibly before then – and was precisely defined by Claude Bernard in the nineteenth. Until about the time of the First World War, people who performed 'vivisections' spoke of themselves quite naturally as 'vivisectors'. The terrible connotations that gathered round these words, however, made them odious in the public mind, and the practitioners ceased to use them. Millions of animals are still being 'vivisected' – in the literal sense – daily in the world's laboratories; but there are no more 'vivisectors'. The word has been expunged from the vocabulary of science. The need was then felt of some new expression that would include this vast infliction of agony without suggesting misery or pain; and it was met by the invention of the current phrase – 'biomedical research'.

Semanticly, this could hardly be improved on, for it covers every variety of investigation into life and medicine; and from the point of view of publicity, since the greater part of this is laudable and the cruel fraction has no separate designation, it is an inspired phrase. So the criminal took sanctuary in the church and disguised himself in a cassock. His pursuers were then placed in a bad light; for to oppose 'vivisection' is humane, but to impede 'biomedical research' is obscurantist. Although the cruel fraction is even greater than it was, any mention of it today is superciliously dismissed as 'a vicious attack on biomedical research.' There has, however, been one odd consequence of the new terminology: since the anti-vivisection societies of Great Britain launched and initially financed the Lawson Tait Memorial Trust, which is a medical charity for research without vivisection, the British Union for the Abolition of Vivisection, the National Anti-Vivisection Society and the Scottish Society for the Prevention of Vivisection have all become active participants in 'biomedical research'.

Distinctions, therefore, are still necessary; and it may be that the old word, although inexact, will have to serve. It is a question of definition; and in the *Survey*, its meaning is illustrated by a list of procedures, for each of which the compilers give a reference in the scientific literature.

'Vivisection [they write] comprises as acts already accomplished:
'Attacking the brain; attacking the spinal cord; stopping natural excretion by tying ducts and like means; grafting diseased matter into the eyes; severing and irritating the nerves; sawing the bones; piercing the bones with a red-hot needle; slow and intermittent suffocation by water, by mercury, by plugging the wind-pipe, by immersing the head in liquid plaster-of-Paris; excising vital organs; burning the foot, the nose, etc., with a Bunsen gas flame; compel-

ling the inhalation of live flame; blasting the open throat with a blow-pipe; producing gastric ulceration; introducing gall-stones into the gall-bladder; inoculating with viruses of various diseases; baking and parboiling; freezing; sewing up the anal canal of pregnant dogs and keeping them thus alive; obstructing womb-outlet in actual labour; blocking up the gullet; distending the stomach with water; preventing sleep.'

Many other procedures have since been devised, and the list lengthens every year. As the statistics prove, it is not in the nature of these things to wither, but to grow.

This is what the anti-vivisection movement is *against*. It is against barbarity. It is consequently *for* humane science; and it is the special virtue of this *Survey* to show that it has received the support of scientists. Those who signed the *Survey* belong with the 'new sowers', and their names form a roll of honour that ought not to be forgotten.

Signatories

Isabel P. Allan, M.B., CH.B.; Bertrand P. Allinson, M.R.C.S., L.R.C.P.; Reginald F. E. Austin, M.R.C.S., L.R.C.P., Major late R.A.M.C.; M. Beddow Bayley, M.R.C.S., L.R.C.P.; R. T. Bowden, M.D., M.R.C.S.; Arthur Case, M.R.C.V.S.; Noel C. Cassal, A.R.C.S., B.SC.; James Clark, B.SC., PH.D.; E. L. Compston, M.B., CH.B.; A. H. Croucher, M.D. (EDIN.), F.R.C.S. (EDIN.); William O'Donnell, L.R.C.P.I., L.R.C.S.I.; H. Tudor Edmunds, M.B., B.S., M.R.C.S., L.R.C.P.; R. Fielding-Ould, M.D., M.R.C.P., M.A.; Andrew Gold, L.R.C.P., L.R.C.S., L.R.F.P.S.; J. Brown Hendry, L.R.C.P., L.R.C.S. (EDIN.); J. Dodson Hessey, M.R.C.S., L.R.C.P.; J. Stenson Hooker, M.D. (DURH.); R. J. Kennard Hope, M.R.C.S., L.R.C.P.; James Horsley, M.B., B.S.; N. L. Joynt, M.B., B.CH.; Catherine Kirk, M.A., M.B., D.P.H.; H. Valentine Knaggs, M.R.C.S., L.R.C.P., L.S.A.; G. W. McAlpine, M.B., CH.B.; N. MacKillop, M.B., CH.B.; Andrew S. McNeil, L.R.C.P., L.R.C.S. (EDIN.); Dorothy Mazel, M.R.C.S.,

L.R.C.P.; Reginald S. Millar, M.R.C.S., L.R.C.P.; H. G. Nicholson, J.P., M.R.C.S., L.S.A.; E. M. J. Paterson, M.B., CH.B., D.P.H.; John Paterson, M.B., CH.B., D.P.H. (CAMB.); Cyril V. Pink, M.R.C.S., L.R.C.P.; Kevin F. Quin, M.R.C.V.S.; Thomas Robertson, M.B., CH.B., B.SC.; L. C. Rowan-Robinson, M.B., CH.B. (EDIN.); C. Stirling Saunder, L.R.C.P. (LOND.); John Shaw, M.D. (LOND.), M.R.C.S.; Bernard Spencer, M.R.C.S., L.R.C.P.; E. H. M. Stancomb, M.B., C.M. (EDIN.); Henry P. Taylor, J.P., M.B., C.M. (ABERD.); G. N. W. Thomas, M.B., CH.B. (EDIN.), D.P.H.; Ethel U. Vawdrey, L.R.C.P., L.R.C.S. (EDIN.), L.F.P.S. (GLAS.); Margaret C. Vivian, L.S.A., L.M.S.S.A. (LOND.); F. J. Wheeler, M.R.C.S., L.R.C.P.; W. H. White, M.R.C.S., L.R.C.P.; H. Fergie Woods, M.D. (BRUX.), M.R.C.S., L.R.C.P.

CHAPTER TWELVE

The Puppet Players

1929 was a year of much interest to the movement. In June, a Labour Government took office; and almost the entire Cabinet were known to be opposed to vivisection. The posts of Prime Minister and Home Secretary were filled by Ramsay MacDonald and J. R. Clynes. Philip Snowden and Arthur Henderson were also ministers. And all four of them, in July 1909, had been vice-presidents of the London Congress of the World League against Vivisection. They had not changed their convictions on the subject. And in 1909, it will be recalled, the congress sponsored by Louise Lind-af-Hageby had also received the support of the whole Parliamentary Labour Party. It was therefore not unnatural that those who had the cause at heart were expectant.

A question and answer in the House of Commons early in July were a disappointment, and one of the anti-vivisection societies consequently sent a reproachful letter to the Home Secretary. His reply concluded as follows:

'I doubt whether any Minister could ever undertake public responsibilities in a Department covering a great variety of work, if in all respects he had to harmonize his public duties with his private opinion.

Yours sincerely, J. R. Clynes.'

This deserves a place in a text-book of politics, and no student of the art should miss it. It could be used as a formula to cover any lapse from the failure to implement a rash election-pledge to the commission of a war-crime. 'As a Minister, I regret that it is impossible for me to harmonize' – what an admirable word –

'my private opinions with my public duties and so . . .' The elasticity is practically infinite.

Clynes had not changed his private opinions on vivisection, nor had his colleagues in the Cabinet; but his conception of public duty was to allow himself to be used, in spite of his beliefs, as a mouth-piece by the officials of the department of which he was in charge. And he was pliant to the full extent of upholding in public the opposite of what he privately considered to be right.

In this way, one may think, good causes are betrayed. But to pillory Clynes in particular would be unfair: it is rather his misfortune to provide an example. He was a well-meaning man; and it requires a very determined new minister to stand up to his permanent officials, even on a matter that may touch his conscience. As his views on this question, and those of the Prime Minister, were well-known, however, both of them were pressed in the House of Commons.

The first occasion, early in July, was a renewed attempt to obtain the exemption of dogs from vivisection. Numerous efforts to this end had been made without success – notably in March 1912 – but the advent of sympathetic ministers had revived hopes for this legislation. Clynes had then given another revealing answer. It was the duty of the government, he said, to be guided by the 'best possible advice'. As no one will dispute that, it raises only one question, By whom is the government advised on this matter? In the first instance, of course, it is by the special department of the Home Office; but Clynes did not mention that. He said that he would not bring in legislation for the exemption of dogs, because the previous government, in 1927, had been advised against it by the Medical Research Council.

It is evident that the Medical Research Council could not have advised anything else. It would never recommend that any right whatsoever that researchers already possess in law should be relinquished. It is the advocate of one party; and its memoranda, as a matter of course, state only one side of the case. It has the right to be heard; but, as Clynes well knew, there are two parties to this suit.

The mere fact that a law exists is sufficient to show that scientific considerations are not the only ones that must be taken into account. If they had been, the whole question would have been left to scientific bodies, and there would have been no reason for society, through parliament, to concern itself with the matter at all. The law is there because there is a recognized conflict of interest; and it is the duty of parliament, acting judicially, to give weight to the claims of both sides.

All this was clearly established in the Report of the first Royal Commission from which the legislation on the subject stems. The Report rejected the argument that science should be the sole judge, and it accepted the need for 'legislative interference'. It laid down in principle that a means must be found of reconciling 'the sentiment of humanity with the desire for scientific knowledge.' And it ended with a definition of what ought to be the spirit of the Act: 'We trust that Your Majesty's Government and the Parliament of this kingdom will recognize the claim of the lower animals to be treated with humane consideration, and will establish the right of the community to be assured that this claim shall not be forgotten amid the triumphs of advancing science.'

'*The sentiment of humanity*' and '*the desire for scientific knowledge*'.

It could not be more plainly stated that there are two parties to the case, and it is laid as a trust on government and parliament to ensure that justice shall be done to both. That was a hundred years ago. How have they performed this trust? Who has been briefed as counsel for Humanity? No one to whom they have been willing to attend. How have they proceeded in their court of justice? They have taken the counsel for the defence as their adviser, and the counsel for the prosecution has been shut out.

It was this situation that determined the answer that Clynes gave in the House of Commons. The government's advisers were – and they still are – purely scientific; they were – and they still are – merely counsel for one party. As long as they remain the government's only advisers, the Act will never be amended in the interest of the other party. If the law is changed at all, it will be in favour of research. This is contrary to the spirit of the Royal Commission's Report, which should have inspired both the original legislation and any subsequent proposal for its amendment. How has it come about?

Coleridge began his magnificent indictment of the Home Office with words equivalent to, 'I accuse!' But in the present context, I should prefer to say, 'I compliment!'

I compliment those persons who have a vested interest in preventing further legislation for the protection of laboratory animals on the skilful wire-pulling by means of which they have manipulated successive governments for nearly a hundred years.

They would seem to have made only one important blunder, and that was so long ago that it has been forgotten. This slip was the letter published in *The British Medical Journal* in April 1882, of which Coleridge made such devastating use in his evidence before the second Royal Commission. The letter, it will be recalled, laid down the strategy and tactics to be followed – namely, not to seek the abolition of the Act, but *'to secure its being harmlessly administered'*, and to bring effectual pressure to bear on officials by *'other means than those which are suited to the arena of controversy.'* In less polished language, the tactics were to be dextrous wire-pulling in Whitehall; and they were so successful that, when Coleridge exposed it in his evidence in 1907, the Association for the Advancement of Medicine by Research had for years been the government's sole advisers.

Some changes were made after this revelation. But what has been their consequence? A new Advisory Committee was set up, but it remained exclusively scientific. And half a century later, in 1957, a Home Secretary (the present Lord Butler) informed Air Chief Marshal Lord Dowding that the government would not lift a finger in this matter without the approval of its advisers.

Surely, then, one ought to compliment the masters of the show for maintaining, since 1888, this superb performance of puppetry.

It is now possible to understand an otherwise inexplicable phenomenon – a government composed almost wholly of anti-vivisectionists defending in parliament the use of dogs for vivisection. It was being guided, according to its Home Secretary, by the 'best possible advice'. The puppets were dancing on the strings. And the newest string, to which Clynes drew the attention of the House, was the 1927 Memorandum.* This was certainly worth recalling. Seldom, one may think, have purely scientific advisers essayed such a flight of oratory.

'It has been [the Memorandum asserted] by the use of dogs that the chief foundations of our knowledge of the processes of digestion, the circulation of lymph, the work of the heart, and the circulation of the blood have been laid. Large and essential parts of our knowledge of the science of feeding are based upon the results of trials made in the feeding of dogs. The work of the surgeon, whether upon the brain and spinal cord, or upon the intestine, or upon the chest, has been made possible by experiments on dogs. Methods of life-saving, as by the transfusion of blood or in the resuscitation of the apparently drowned, have been worked out chiefly by trials with dogs. Important parts of our knowledge of anaesthetics and their safe administration, and of the actions of many kinds of drugs, have been gained by the experimental use of dogs. There is no medical practitioner who does not use in his daily work information which he owes to experiments upon dogs. If he is to understand the meaning of such common symptoms as palpitation, breathlessness, giddiness, fainting, and many other forms of distress, if he feels a pulse or listens to a chest, if he transfuses his patient with blood, or employs rectal feeding, he is

* Memorandum upon the Dogs Protection Bill, issued by the Medical Research Council, June 7, 1927.

making wholesale use of knowledge derived from experiments upon unconscious dogs.'

It is not surprising that Clynes found this unsurpassable; and certainly no one who is conversant with the literature of vivisection will deny that innumerable atrocities have been perpetrated on dogs. Its pages are clamorous with the barking, whining, yelping, howling of fully-conscious dogs; and its annals are punctuated by the complaints, legal actions, and even physical assaults made by the outraged neighbours of some infamous laboratories. The Memorandum does not mention these things, but it recalls them to knowledgeable minds. Its claims, however, are not the practitioner's account of the foundations of his science; and not even the vanished bedside manner of a politer age would reassure the patient who was solemnly informed, 'Everything we know is derived from experiments on dogs.'

To the experimentalist, of course, the patient's feelings are beside the point; and it would certainly appear from its Memorandum that if the Medical Research Council were deprived of its dogs, it would be out of work. So it would seem, but the truth may be otherwise: it may even be that humane methods of research would have led to greater employment and better therapeutics. At all events, the Council had the right to put the case for science; and the government had the duty to listen with equal attention to the case for humanity.

To whom might they have turned for this? It might have been to the Sovereign, who has a constitutional right 'to advise and warn', and so they might have remembered that Queen Victoria once wrote to her Prime Minister expressing the hope that he would speak strongly against vivisection, which she described as 'a disgrace to humanity and Christianity.' Or they might have recalled the many pleas of Lord Shaftesbury, and the occasion when he said in the House of Lords, after describing an experiment, 'I would infinitely rather have been the dog than the professor.' There are many other distinguished people to whom they might have turned; but on this particular question, a Bill for the exemption of dogs, perhaps their best adviser would have been John Galsworthy, who had written on the matter when a similar Bill had been introduced fifteen years earlier. He had then said:

'Even if it be granted that the dog, by reason of its intelligence and nervous organization, is more fitted than other animals for certain vivisectional experiments (though I believe this is disputed), there are yet basic considerations which make such treatment of the dog a scandalous betrayal. Man, no doubt, first bound and bred the dog to his service and companionship for purely utilitarian reasons; but we of today, by immemorial tradition and a sentiment that has become almost as inherent in us as the sentiment towards children, give him a place in our lives utterly different from that which we accord to any other animal (not even excepting cats); a place that he has won for himself throughout the ages, and that he ever increasingly deserves. He is by far the nearest thing to man on the face of the earth; the one link that we have spiritually with the animal creation; the one dumb creature into whose eyes we can look and tell pretty well for certain what emotion, even what thought is at work within; the one dumb creature which – not as a rare exception, but almost always – steadily feels the sentiments of love and trust. This special nature of the dog is . . . extraordinarily precious even to those of us who profess to be without sentiment. It is one of the prime factors in our daily lives in all classes of society, this mute partnership with dogs; and – we are still vivisecting them!

'I am told that pro-vivisectionists are fighting tooth and nail against the Bill (now in committee stage in the House of Commons) which has for object the exemption of dogs from all vivisectional and inoculative experiments. If it indeed be so, I ask them: "Would you, any one of you, give up your own dog to the vivisector's knife, or respect the man who gave or sold you his dog for your experiments?" I take it they would reply: "We would not give our own dogs. We should think poorly of the man who sold or gave us his dog. The dogs we use are homeless, masterless dogs." And in turn I would answer: "There are no dogs born in this country without home or master. The dogs you use are those who have already fallen on cruelty or misfortune, whom as kindly men you pity or should pity; these are the dogs, the lost dogs that you take for your experiments, to make their ends more wretched than their lives have been."

'If this be sentiment, it is not mere cultured sentiment, but based on a very real and simple sense of what is decent... We all have this feeling; yet, when for our own alleged benefit we want to violate it, we can still say: "Oh, it does not matter; this dog is already down." In a word, what we would not do with our own dogs we have no right to do with the dogs that have not had the luck to be ours. It is not so much a question of love of dogs as of good faith in man...

'I am not concerned to discuss the disputed question of whether or not special benefit does arise from experiments on dogs... After all, we are not only bodies but spirits, and when our minds have once become alive to ethical doubt on a question such as this (there are 870,000 signatures on a petition for the total exemption of dogs from vivisection) when we are no longer sure that we have the right so to treat our dog comrades, there has fallen a shadow on the human conscience that will surely grow, until, by adjustment of our actions to our ethical sense, it has been remedied.'*

The shadow has spread across the earth since that was written: everywhere we are buying knowledge at the price of justice and mercy, and so forfeiting our right to happiness. Can this be the outcome of taking the 'best possible advice'? Let Galsworthy's letter stand as the case for *'the sentiment of humanity'* and the Council's Memorandum as that for *'the desire for scientific knowledge.'* Does anyone feel certain that in ignoring the

* John Galsworthy: *A Sheaf*, Heinemann, 1916, pp. 64–69.

one and listening only to the other our governments were wise?

'A scandalous betrayal,' was Galsworthy's opinion. If he was right, we have darkened the human spirit; and that cannot lead to human good. Knowledge is two-edged, and it depends on the character of those who have it whether it is a blessing or a curse.

* * *

The case as Galsworthy expressed it is one that should command the attention of any government, but it would have been too much to expect of the majority of governments that they should listen to Bernard Shaw. The Labour Government of 1929, however, ought to have been an exception; because Shaw, as a veteran Fabian, had for long been a close friend of many of its ministers; and all of them knew that the political principles to which they were most committed had been advanced and some perhaps even fathered by Shaw with a seriousness that was in no way diminished by the coruscations of his wit. In 1927, the year of the Memorandum, he had written something on the question which these future ministers had no doubt read at the time, and might have been expected to remember. As it affords probably the last smile that this book will have to offer, it shall be remembered here.

From the eighteen-nineties until his death after the Second World War, Shaw served the anti-vivisection movement with zeal. For more than half a century, he was its self-appointed court-jester; and it owes him a debt for the moments when it was surprised by laughter. To be both entertaining and compassionate is a rare achievement, but Shaw often was. He was always the better for a good adversary, and this was sometimes supplied by his old friend H. G. Wells. Wells supported vivisection, and they often wrangled on the subject. In the summer of 1927, Wells wrote an article defending vivisection in *The Sunday Express*. Shaw made a point-by-point reply, and this gave him the opportunity of saying a memorable last word:

'But Mr Wells has another shot in his locker ... "There is a residuum of admittedly painful cases, but it is an amount of suffering infinitessimal in comparison with the gross aggregate of pain inflicted day by day upon sentient creatures by mankind."

'This defence fits every possible crime from pitch-and-toss to manslaughter. Its disadvantage is that it is not plausible enough to impose on the simplest village constable. Even Landru, and the husband of the brides in the bath, though in desperate peril of the guillotine and the gallows, had not the effrontery to say: "It is true that we made our livelihood by marrying women and burning them in the stove or drowning them in the bath when we had spent their money; and we admit frankly and handsomely that the process may have involved some pain and disillusionment for them; but their sufferings (if any) were infinitessimal in comparison with the gross aggregate of pain inflicted day by day upon sentient creatures by mankind." Landru and Smith knew what Wells forgot: that scoundrels who have no better defence than that have no defence at all ...

'The Anti-Vivisector does not deny that physiologists must make experiments and even take chances with new methods. He says they must not seek knowledge by criminal methods, just as they must not make money by criminal methods. He does not object to Galileo dropping cannon balls from the top of the leaning tower of Pisa; but he would object to shoving off two dogs, or two American tourists.'*

The Labour Ministers of 1929 might have remembered this, others could hardly have been expected to do so; but every government has the duty to listen to both sides of the case of Humanity *versus* Science. In addition, one may think, there are some political obligations. It was the Conservative Party which introduced the original legislation in 1876; and since that time, our laws in every

* Reproduced by kind permission of *The Sunday Express*.

field of welfare have been greatly improved. It might therefore be expected of a modern Conservative government that it should amend this outmoded Act, in accordance with the others, in the spirit of humaneness. And the Labour Party, which has promised so much and performed nothing, might well be asked, 'What has happened to the ideals of 1909?'

CHAPTER THIRTEEN

John Cowper Powys

In the summer of 1933, John Cowper Powys was sixty. He was then living in an isolated cottage in the State of New York, finishing his autobiography and suffering from a gastric ulcer. It was a hot, dry summer, and the neighbouring stream had been reduced to a string of pools. In spite of heat, work and pain, he used to go down to the stream-bed, catch the fish in the small pools in a butterfly-net, put them in a bucket of water and carry them to the large pools. 'Our brook is dry,' he wrote in a letter, 'and this rescuing of fish is a burden, not only when I'm doing it, but on conscience when I'm not.'

Powys was doomed to have a conscience of some sort, because his father, both grandfathers, and one great-grandfather had all been clergymen; but it did not have to be one of this sort. His was not a clerical conscience: on the surface, it seemed more like Shaw's, due to a widening of the sense of fellow-feeling; but in Powys there were depths below that. He was profoundly aware of his kinship with life, almost to the point of mystical participation. And this led him to suggest a restatement of the Christian commandment to love one's neighbour: 'I would substitute,' he wrote, 'Thou shalt be merciful and pitiful and compassionate to all living organisms.'

He believed himself to be a born actor; but his acting, like his conscience, was carried a step beyond what is usual. It enabled him to assume and feel any part in nature, by means of 'those imaginative nerves which compel us to identify our own feelings with those of an alien existence.' It is these imaginative nerves that stir the sympathies and awaken the sense of cosmic involvement from which great art derives. Powys possessed them, as Blake did, to an extent that some may think pathological. Excess is possible in anything; but without this sense of participation, which is a mode of knowledge, there would be no major art. All poets – and many who are poets by nature although not in achievement – have this sense, as when Keats describes watching trees in the wind and feeling that his whole inner being was stirred, tossed and wind-blown.

People who are conscious of this resonance, this involvement, need no argument to condemn the cruelties of research. They experience them. 'They have made the whole earth a wilderness for me,' wrote Anna Kingsford, 'and my whole life one long struggle and protest.' Powys understood that. He discovered what he calls 'the cruel curiosity of science' when he was at Cambridge, early in the 1890s, and he immediately judged it to be 'an abominable crime against the only morality that is worth a fig, a crime committed not only against animals, but against everything that is noblest in ourselves.'*

The discovery of vivisection was one of the severest psychological shocks of his early manhood, and remained a tormenting preoccupation to the end of his days. In his autobiography, written forty years after, he says that it 'outraged – and continues to outrage – something in my deepest being.' For him, the justification for this sense of outrage was a living truth, one that no argument had induced and that none could confute. 'My knowledge that the practice of vivisection is a crime against all that is noblest in our race is not a conviction, *it is my life*.' He was familiar with the claims of the apologists, but they left him unmoved. 'With my whole being *I know*, I answer them, that the vivisecting of dogs is evil ... That is really how we all know that all evil is evil. You can find reasons to defend anything.'†

Others have served this cause by eloquence and argument as well as Powys, but he made one contribution to it that is unique. On

---

* John Cowper Powys, *Autobiography*, Macdonald, ed. 1967, p. 192, reproduced here by kind permission of the Estate of the Late John Cowper Powys.
† Ibid. p. 200–01.

account of his own experience, but experience of quite another character, he was able to shed at least some light on the darkest of its recesses.

'Without question [he says in his autobiography] from earliest childhood up to the present hour, my dominant vice has been the most dangerous of all vices. I refer to Sadism. I cannot remember a time – so early did this tendency show itself – when sadistic thoughts and images did not disturb and intoxicate me. One of my picture-books, when I could not have been more than three years old, contained a picture of an eagle seizing upon a lamb; and from the age of three, that is to say from the year 1875 – for I was born in 1872 – till about the year 1922, when I was fifty, this deadly vice transported and obsessed me... It was not till I was fifty, and that date remains very clear in my mind, that I entirely overcame it. By "overcoming" it I mean never allowing myself to derive pleasure even for a moment in those sadistic thoughts which were my bosom houris, the attendants at my pillow, for nearly half a century.

'For the last ten years my Conscience – finding no doubt the temptation more within its power to resist – has been so rigid with me that it has compelled me even to skip those passages in modern books, and they are many, which play upon the sadistic nerve. I doubt if there is any reader of books in England or America with a more infallible wand than I for detecting the various degrees of sadism in a writer...

'It is not that I ever practised – no! not in the smallest degree – the sadistic actions that I was always thinking about... No, it is in my thoughts that I have devoured – to dark ecstasy to dark ecstasy – this sweet, abominable Dead Sea fruit.'*

It may seem paradoxical that a sadist should be one of the most compassionate of men. But sadism is not simply a synonym for cruelty. It is a sexual deviation; and, as such, it may seem not less

* Ibid. p. 8.

but more terrible, not less but more to be combated, to those who have it than to those who are immune.

No one, however, can be completely immune to any deviation. It is a question of circumstance whether it is developed or not. A psychiatrist would seek its roots in childhood, and so expose the social as well as the personal aspect of the problem. Sadism and masochism are grounded in feelings of insecurity and inadequacy; and they afford compensations, through abnormal relationships, in which the individual does feel sure of himself and his powers. Such compensations begin in day-dreams, that may be either of exaggerated aggression or utter subjugation. These phantasies of childhood are seeds from which sado-masochism may afterwards develop—the seeds, that is to say, of what is, in its extreme forms, the most terrible of all deviations, that in which erotic satisfaction is related to giving or receiving pain. This is not mere brutality. It is liable to occur in people who are imaginatively gifted, as was the Marquis de Sade himself. Intellectual qualities afford no protection. And as almost no child achieves a perfect balance between self and society, the danger is common. If the tendency is established, this risk becomes a misfortune; and if it is expressed, the misfortune becomes a crime.

More pornographic literature is devoted to sadism and masochism than to any other deviations; many forms of entertainment are tinged by them; and there is no doubt that sadism may be fostered by vivisection. It was not a fanatical humanitarian, but a professor of surgery at Harvard who once observed, 'Watch the students at a vivisection. It is the blood and suffering, not the science, that rivets their breathless attention.'* If there were no other reasons for making vivisection illegal, this would be enough. If sadistic tendencies which might otherwise remain dormant are awakened in youth by a teaching authority under the aegis of science, it breaks down the greatest safeguard against their further development – the sense of guilt. If education itself makes cruelty

* Henry J. Biglow, quoted by Leffingwell, op. cit. p. 45.

acceptable, a childish phantasy will easily become an adult vice. The professors who introduce their students to this practice have no conception of the harm they do, but that does not make it any less. 'My own experience of life,' Powys wrote, 'has taught me that when Jesus prayed that his tormentors might be forgiven because they knew not what they did, he prayed for the most wicked and dangerous people in the world.'*

Out of his own experience, Powys was able to speak with a unique authority. Many others have stated that sadism is relevant to any serious discussion of vivisection, and some of them may have shared his knowledge of it; but no one else has had the courage to admit to such an intimate understanding. From the social standpoint, however, this neglected aspect is very grave; and during his long sojourn in America, where vivisection is practised far more than in Europe, Powys came to the conclusion that this is the greatest crime of modern man:

'The public in America has been kept in the dark, even more than the public in England, about this matter of vivisection . . . *Totally unnecessary cruelty* on a scale that the general public has no conception of, is going on all the while. The word "science" covers every kind of atrocity, and the issue is perfectly clear. My opposition to vivisection, particularly the vivisection of dogs, is based upon an argument that is unanswerable. This wickedness contradicts and cancels out the one single advantage that our race has got from what is called evolution, namely the development of our sense of right and wrong. If vivisection, as it is increasingly practised by these unscrupulous, pitiless, unphilosophical scientists, is allowed to go on unchecked . . . something that the mysterious forces of the universe have themselves developed in us will soon have its spiritual throat cut to the bone.'†

Having reached this conclusion, Powys not unnaturally regarded

* John Cowper Powys, op. cit. p. 113.
† Ibid. pp. 639–40.

the cruelty of science as the lineal successor to the legal and religious cruelties of former centuries; he saw the sworn tormentor, the inquisitor, and the vivisector as one devil in three majestic cloaks – law, religion and science; and unless this devil was exposed and driven out, he believed that the human spirit would be eclipsed.

Some people will think this excessive, but it explains why Powys himself was convinced that the noblest of his emotions was 'a prophetic anger against all scientists who vivisect dogs.' The key word is 'prophetic'. He foresaw a day of retribution for science and for man, and this led him to the composition of one of the most curious works of modern literature. It does not realize his intentions with complete success, but nothing he wrote reveals him more clearly than *Morwyn* as 'a great original'.

Morwyn was published in 1937, and Aldous Huxley's *Ends and Means* appeared in the following year. Looking back, the date seems appropriate; because although one is imaginative and the other rationalistic, both, in a sense, are menacing, prophetic books.

CHAPTER FOURTEEN

The Myth of 'Morwyn'

To build a bridge of pure reason from the earth to the stars, to penetrate the secrets of the sun, to look up at the Alps and know that their dawn-touched summits were lifted from the bed of a vanished sea, to understand the evolution of life and our kinship, cousinship, with all its forms – these are triumphs and revelations that we owe to science, and that have given, or that might give, new joys to life.

These splendid gifts, and the likelihood of further gifts, make it all the more grievous that science as we have it today should have been so spoilt, overshadowed and shamed by the cruelty of some of its most eulogized figures that there have been men of genius in a different sphere, overcome by revulsion and disgust, who have seen no good whatever in science and have regarded it as something to be hated and feared.

This reaction is extreme, but it cannot be dismissed. On the contrary, it is a part of the charge against contemporary scientists that men of eminence in other fields should have been brought to this extremity. Powys is one example. His world was darkened by these cruelties, and he writes of them with a bitterness that may appear to be obsessive. But others have suffered at least as much; and one laboratory-visitor in the United States felt life to be so devalued by what she had seen that she took her own. Obsession and suicide are not commendable; but these instances would not have happened without a cause. The extraordinary novel in which Powys is chiefly concerned with this underlying evil may not rank as a great work of literature; but it is, at least, an important literary curiosity, and it is a book that no reader will forget.

When science-fiction created a new kind of phantasy, it dealt a severe, but not quite deadly blow to a much older literary form. From *The Book of the Dead* and *The Epic of Gilgamesh*, from *The Odyssey*, *The Aeneid* and *The Divine Comedy* to *Faust*, with Goethe's prologue in heaven and Berlioz' ballet in hell, journeys to some other world, Elysian Fields or Land of Shades, have been a conspicuous part of the literary tradition. Science-fiction and such works of poetic seership are, in a sense, complementary forms; because both aim to draw out and exhibit as a future – the one physically on this or some other planet, and the other psychically in heaven or hell – some implication of our present state. Both are likely to open with a strange journey, either by space-craft to a remote region of the world-body, or by means of some spell or token into the recesses of the world-soul.

The spirit of our age virtually forbids anyone to write a new *Divine Comedy*. Paradise has become inaccessible. But hell is more easily approached; and in offering us, two years before the Second World War, a new version of hell, Powys responded to the contemporary spirit. *Morwyn* is a modern myth, relating the adventures of four characters, one of them a dog, in the underworld. This hell has its traditional location in the depths of the earth; and the approach to it is made rather uneasily, owing something to Homer and the other poets and something to Jules Verne. Hell is entered, in this novel, through a mountain in Wales.

It is the shortest day of the year. Dusk is falling. The characters are climbing a narrow mountain-path, which compels them to walk in single file. Morwyn's father leads the way. He is a distinguished man of science, engaged in biomedical research. We are never told his name: he is referred to simply as the Vivisector. Morwyn comes next; then the narrator, also unnamed but unmistakably Powys; and lastly his dog, Black Peter. The reader feels that this order is symbolic, but in what sense is at first obscure: later, when the destination is disclosed, it becomes clear why the procession is led by the Vivisector. He is a rational man, but he does not know – none of them knows – whither they are heading. His daughter follows him from what aspires to be a redemptive love; the narrator follows her from satyrish desire; and Black Peter, although apprehensive of hell and terrified of the Vivisector, follows his master from simple fidelity. Ripples of allusion spread back into ancient mythology, and they have implications, also, for the future of man. These are often confusing; but it gradually becomes clear that Morwyn and Black Peter are to be seen as types of innocence, and the Vivisector as a symbol of damned humanity.

When they reach the top of the mountain, a mysterious, menacing change comes over everything. It is partly physical, as if a thunderstorm were brewing, and partly psychical, conferring, even on Black Peter, an abnormal lucidity. It is a horrifying experience, as if some ghastly crack had opened in the surface of nature to disclose unsuspected depths. Then the mountain is struck by what seems to be a meteorite – 'a colossal bolt hurled at our little oasis of order out of the blind tumult of outer chaos' – and the whole rocky mass on which they are standing is driven by its impact into the bowels of the earth. The narrator, Morwyn and Black Peter are not killed. The Vivisector is struck physically dead, but this does not extinguish his personality, or even modify it in any noticeable way. His death makes virtually no difference; except that in the underworld, into which they have all been plunged, he is now a resident spirit, while the others are expatriated travellers.

We shall not follow their adventures, but consider only the author's intentions. Powys did not write his books with the aim of giving entertainment or creating works of art. They may display both qualities incidentally, but he designed them to be propaganda for his idiosyncratic philosophy. There is an anti-intellectual element in this which makes it recalcitrant to reasoned exposition; but the title of Professor Wilson Knight's book on Powys describes it aptly——*The Saturnian Quest*. The meaning of this is disclosed in *Morwyn*.

Saturn was the god of the Golden Age. Although he and his

kingdom have now vanished from the world, he is not dead. At the heart of things – symbolically expressed in *Morwyn* as a cave at the centre of the earth – Saturn sleeps. This holy cavern lies underneath the Powys hell, and the sleeping god there is like a seed or promise of Earth's ultimate redemption. When he wakes, his kingdom will be restored; and the hope of the Powys faith therefore lies in the fulfilment of the Virgilian prophecy – *redeunt Saturnia regna*.

The Golden Age was lost through man's wickedness; and Powys appears to have taken his definition of wickedness from Walter Savage Landor: 'Cruelty is the chief, if not the only sin.' This simplifies his eschatology, and his hell contains none of the fine gradations of offence that are to be found in Dante. Most of the crimes that are dealt with in the law-courts on earth do not lead to it: cruelty alone demands damnation. There are nonetheless degrees among the damned; and these are represented in order of intensifying evil by the symbolic shades of the Marquis de Sade, the Grand Inquisitor, and the Vivisector – erotic cruelty, religious cruelty, and scientific cruelty.

The Marquis de Sade, who acts as first guide to the party, is the least of these offenders; because erotic cruelty is only occasional, and his was partly expiated in prison on earth. It is those who have escaped justice altogether above who are in the worst state below, but they are not being punished in the theological sense. The System-of-Things, which is the Powys equivalent to God, has for its ultimate aim the evolution of sympathy and pity. In the meantime, it is permissive; and the damned suffer through being what they are. Down here, they do what they like; and hell is therefore the gradual creation of all the sadists who have ever lived. In fact it is a human invention; and as all human inventions tend to become more efficient with the passing of time, so hell is becoming more hellish. The Marquis de Sade explains to the travellers.

'It has taken us a long time to make this place as we wanted it. There was an Elysium here in Homer's time. Huge fields of bog-asphodel used to grow here then. Even in Dante's time it still had patches of emerald green grass where philosophers and poets could walk up and down without disturbance. It wasn't until vivisection reached its present point that we could get rid of these archaisms... The System-of-Things goes blindly on with its unscientific evolution of pity and sympathy, and it doesn't bother *us*. *We* don't go blindly on! We are scientists and rationalists.'*

Powys, who borrowed freely from others, may owe something in this novel to the opinion of Bernard Shaw that the vivisector is the worst of scoundrels – partly because he is insatiable, however many facts he may have discovered there will always be others that he does not know, and partly because he is a scoundrel on principle. Doing evil on principle is, at all events, one of the themes of the Powys hell; and it is first announced to the horrified Morwyn by the shades of the Grand Inquisitor and her father, between whom an infernal understanding is soon established.

' "We *must* be cruel for the sake of human souls, lady!" cried the Inquisitor.
' "We *must* be cruel for the sake of human bodies, girl!" echoed the Vivisector.
' "We get knowledge of God when we burn his Image!" cried the Theologian.
' "We get knowledge of Nature when we crucify her children!" echoed the Scientist.
'With this the two obsessed spirits rushed off together...
' "You see what they are!" whispered the Marquis de Sade in my ear. "Their fanatacism has fixed its roots so deeply in cruelty, that you can't separate the two things. I understand the phenomenon perfectly! The abstract thought 'The Pursuit of Truth', and the abstract thought 'The Protection of Truth', no sooner enter

---

* John Cowper Powys: *Morwyn*, Cassell, 1937, p. 65, reproduced here by kind permission of the Estate of the Late John Cowper Powys.

their brain than that nerve which I know so well begins quivering like an aspen, and Monseigneur sees heretics in the flames while Monsieur sees dogs strapped down at his mercy. And the interesting thing is that though persons of my peculiar cult have – it's no use denying it – caused a moity, a quota, a percentage of human anguish, they have been innocent babes compared with these protectors and pursuers of Truth.'"*

The Marquis may have expected damnation, but the Grand Inquisitor and the Vivisector had not. They had been honoured while on earth, and had supposed that they were fooling the System-of-Things. But they had been wrong. The System-of-Things has set its will on the evolution of pity and sympathy, it is against all cruelty, and it has revealed its will in the human conscience. An individual or a society may stifle conscience; but in that case it will be damned, and eventually, through being opposed to the cosmic will, it will be destroyed. This explains the sub-title of *Morwyn – The Vengeance of God*; and it exhibits the grounds of 'prophetic anger'. The Powysian prophecy is the damnation and destruction of the present world-order, which is dominated by cruelty. After that, those who are aware of the cosmic purpose, and of what is and always has been the goal of evolution, will create a new world-order of mercy and justice.

This will coincide with the awakening of Saturn; but in the meantime, the rise of vivisection is bringing hell to its own peculiar ripeness as a place of subtle and remorseless evil, and it now forms a great bond between the living and the damned. Here, where the lost souls of cruelty are gathered, the favourite pastime is to watch the television screens, which show what is happening in the vivisection laboratories of the upper world. It is a ceaseless programme, and draws crowds of agitated shadows. They are described as a 'swarming multitude of tantalized spirits which heaved and twisted like a seething mass of tadpoles, newly emerged from their natal

* Ibid. pp. 77–78.

spawn, or like millions of shining maggots making of themselves a living fountain of corruption.' Nothing has given so much satisfaction in hell as this, or done more to further its purposes. 'To torture for knowledge,' the spirit of the Marquis exclaimed in admiration, 'why, the devil himself must have invented that beautiful idea! It cuts at the very root of right and wrong. To burn alive to save souls was a happy inspiration; but this baking and freezing alive for pure knowledge – why it undermines the moral evolution of twenty thousand years!'*

The infernal landscape owes something to Dante, something to Jules Verne, and occasionally suggests a Bacon painting. Beneath a sky of stone, there is a plain of rock which ends at the brink of an abyss. The stench that rises from this gulf makes the travellers think they are descending into the 'Morgue of the Universe'. At its bottom they discover a sinister sea, and crouched beside its dark waters, bending over them, two monstrous shapes.

'They were looking downwards with what seemed to me, from where I stood, almost human lineaments. These lineaments were only in half-profile, for the larger portion of their cyclopean physiognomies were turned seaward, but no words of mine, my good son, can describe the horror of their expression! I thought to myself, as I stared in stupefied awe, that no one could have looked upon their full faces and survived such a Gorgonian experience. And, moreover, as I continued to gaze upon them, it seemed to me that there was something else round and about them that touched a limit of frightfulness beyond what they were in themselves. It seemed to me that there floated round them moving images of unspeakable and unbearable cruelty, such as might have curdled the phantom-blood even of our pursuers. The Shapes themselves ... were hunched and humped and indrawn, as if they shrank in undying loathing from the very images of intolerable cruelty

* Ibid. p. 100.

about them, over which, at the same time, they were gloating with an everlasting obsession.'*

Before they had reached this sink of the world, the travellers had found another guide. He was not an inmate of hell, but a visiting spirit; and, to their intense relief, a noble one. He was the Welsh bard, Taliesin. A quest of his own was leading him to explore the recesses of the world-soul; and it was he who explained the humped, crouching figures, half material, half mental, which seemed as if they were being moulded by the breath of the hovering images around them. They were the twin gods of perverted religion and obsessed science – the ideal counterparts, one might say, of the Grand Inquisitor and the Vivisector.

'I think', said Taliesin, 'that in the end under the washing of this sea they will become one figure with two faces. They're both, as you observe, still in the process of creation. They're the creation of their worshippers and have only a dim half-life.'

These half-living, growing idols still have a future of uncertain length, but they are nonetheless doomed. They are situated in the nethermost part of hell, but hell is not the foundation of the world. There is a sphere below hell, symbolized by the caves of sleep, which holds the secret of the earth's regeneration. The slumbering Saturn is not the only inmate of these holy caverns; but Powysian mythology, which is at least as much Celtic as Greek, will not be unravelled here. There is one other personage, however, who requires mention: this is Rhadamanthus, who was once reputed to be the perfect judge.

Unlike Saturn, he is not asleep; but he has been stricken with the dreadful gift of immortal life without immortal youth. He is seated behind a cauldron—one of the Celtic elements in the story—in a condition of deathless senility. His intentions are still

* Ibid. p. 168–69.

good, but his strength has left him. His reputation survives, but few now seek his dotard justice. While the travellers gaze at him on his judgment-seat, however, a unique plaintiff suddenly appears. It is a laboratory monkey. It is in a pitiable condition; but by some miracle it has managed to escape, and has reached this world-renowned Court of Justice to plead for the thousands of millions of creatures that science has caged.

'The monkey's disfigured body quivered and shook, and a human voice began to mingle with its pitiful wail; but this gouged-out and scraped-out phantom of a shredded husk, that once in its natural body had swung free among golden boughs, must have felt that it was on the verge of being swallowed up in that vast gulf of black Nothingness, in which the shrillest screams are silenced, and must have resolved to break its cracked heart in one culminating appeal.

' "Judge, Judge!" it shrieked, while its small hands clung desperately to the edge of the Cauldron, just as its perishing consciousness clung to the edge of extinction, "there's a cry going up from these places of torment, a wail of nethermost despair, such as no martyrs at the stake have ever uttered! These, oh just and righteous Judge, had paradise and glory to look for, but we have nothing – nothing, nothing, nothing, nothing! Think not because we are dumb that we lack the feelings of your branch of our race. Closed in our cages, behind those great walls of stone, none can hear our screams but those who cause them. No Heaven, no Jesus, have we to look for when the torment is over. Even Inquisition prisoners, even political prisoners, have a faint hope that one day they may escape. We have no hope. None is ever seen alive again that crosses a vivisection threshold ... The sight of what they reduce us to would turn all but scientific stomachs sick with nausea and shame. At first we can hardly believe that human beings can be such fiends. Hunters and wild beasts we have known, and the brutality of trappers; but this is another thing ... We ourselves have killed and eaten in the struggle for life. But this is different. This is not a matter of life and death. This is not a matter of ancient custom. This is not a primary impulse of nature. *This is pure mental evil!* This is the cold-blooded substitution of the law of evil for the law of good! O Judge, O stern and righteous Judge, hear me this once, this once, before I die for ever! Even if out of our torment their race does prolong its life, is not that life under a curse? Their scientists think they can mock at God, mock at right and wrong, mock at good and evil. They say their ways of cruelty are the law of the universe. O rise up, great and righteous Judge, and condemn these demons, so that the poor creatures of the earth may be avenged!" '*

The dotard Judge says nothing. The little monkey falls into the Cauldron and disappears.

In this age of tyranny, justice is dumb; but one thing that cannot be silenced is the voice of prophecy. The prophet in this story is Taliesin, who had previously intervened at its most dramatic moment. It had then seemed as if Morwyn and Black Peter, the types of innocence, were about to be sacrificed; because the two arch-fanatics had made a compact that if the Grand Inquisitor might have the girl to burn for human souls, then the Vivisector should have the dog for the good of human bodies. A vast concourse of the damned had assembled for this spectacle.

'What will you do with it?' they shrieked.

The chant with which Morwyn's father answered them was seemingly inspired by the list of experimental procedures that is set out in Dr Searle's pamphlet, *A Survey of the Case against Vivisection*. Powys has simply turned part of this passage into the poetry of hell. In his story, however, Morwyn and Black Peter are saved by Taliesin. Although the bard's power lies only in his seership, the legion of threatening spirits shrink back in fear when he prophesies.

* Ibid. p. 228.

We, of course, see through this transparent fiction, and know that the prophecy relates to us:

> 'The vengeance of Heaven will fall upon your race! More will perish because of Science than will live because of it. You can't mock God for ever. The lives you save – if you do save them – will survive to curse you and your diabolical science. The law of the universe is righteousness and justice and mercy and pity: and not all the science in your laboratories can make wrong right. The moan that rises from your places of torment will return upon you and upon your children – yea! it is doing so already! – with a vengeance that will shake the world. It is the pity of God that lies bound upon your tables; it is the justice of God that lies helpless on your racks. It will be the vengeance of God that will descend upon your children's children; for unto them that use the pain of the helpless to extract knowledge, their knowledge shall turn to madness and destruction; and to them that use the torture of the helpless to prolong life, life shall be a burden and a plague and a despair!'*

As a modern scenario of hell, *Morwyn* is without competitor; and it is also an epitome of the Saturnian quest. According to Powys, the cosmic will is set upon a fulfilment of life, *all life*, in a Golden Age that cannot fail; but at present, Saturn sleeps, Justice is impotent, a hoard of menacing phantoms pursues the innocent, and Truth speaks in 'prophetic anger'.

---

* Ibid. pp. 205–06.

CHAPTER FIFTEEN

The Explosion

'Let the public trust the scientists, and trust them fully.'

The speaker was a former President of the British Medical Association, and the context was an address, attacking the antivivisection movement, delivered in 1927. The words are persuasive, seductive, but they should be weighed with care; for when the Serpent of Eden glided to the Tree of Knowledge and enwrapped it in his coils, such was the spirit of his advice.

Knowledge, progress. The growth of knowledge is certain, but there can be few more dangerous illusions than that of the inevitability of progress. Looking back on our tragic century, the opening decade now seems like the Indian Summer of a civilization; but almost everyone who was living then believed that it was Spring.

The First World War, in Lord Allenby's words, 'was a lengthy period of general insanity.' Society never fully recovered from it, and the Second World War was accompanied by a regression in civilized standards throughout the world. We have not yet taken the full measure of this disaster. Few people would have believed, when the century opened, that the enormities of Hitler and Stalin would be possible in civilized Europe; and surely no British Government in Victorian or Edwardian times would have consented to the strategy proposed in the 'Cherwell Minute' which was laid before the War Cabinet in March 1942. What the Minute advocated was area bombing – 'terror bombing' as it has come to be known – which meant that the targets should be neither military nor industrial, but densely-populated residential areas; and it 'envisaged the complete destruction of forty-three selected

German towns ... which had a total population of some fifteen millions.'*

There was a cogent reason for this strategy; because it had been found that the night-bomber could not be used as a rapier, but only as a bludgeon. It remains true, none the less, that to employ it as such was to abandon civilized restraint, and that terror bombing did in fact culminate in the destruction of Dresden and the nuclear obliteration of the cities of Japan. One may reasonably believe that no British Government at the beginning of the century would have agreed to this policy, nor, of course, could it then have been carried out; and that is a stark reminder of the greatest danger of our time – an immense increase in knowledge with no comparable progress in ethics. The advance of science, so far from assuring the advance of civilization, may constitute the chief temptation, almost a compulsion at times, to behave barbarically.

As the Second World War is recent history, it may be desirable to state clearly that this book has no nationalistic undertones. They would be alien to its purpose, which is to draw attention to a world-wide crime against our simpler fellow mortals. There are many ways, of course, in which the dark side of human nature finds expression in the dark face of science; but this book will be restricted to its subject, and the wider context will be recalled only when there is a special reason for doing so. Certain events of the Second World War provide a compelling reason. For many years humanitarians had been giving a warning, well-expressed by Frances Cobbe, that a society that does not check cruelty in science 'may count upon seeing it burst out sooner or later in acts of savage barbarity to men, women and children.' She was derided at the time. And it is, therefore, only just to record that what she and others said would happen did happen.

* * *

* Sir Charles Webster & Nobel Frankland, *The Strategic Air Offensive against Germany*, H.M. Stationery Office, 1961, Vol. I, p. 182.

On the ninth of December 1946, twenty-two men and one woman stood in the dock at the Palace of Justice in Nuremberg. Twenty of them held degrees in medicine, and the proceedings have therefore come to be known as *The Medical Case*.* They were being tried by a United States Military Tribunal, and the opening speech was made by the Chief Counsel for the Prosecution, Brigadier General Telford Taylor. It was a long speech, and in the course of it he said:

'The defendants in this case are charged with murders, tortures, and other atrocities committed in the name of medical science. The victims of these crimes are numbered in hundreds of thousands. A handful only are still alive; a few survivors will appear in this courtroom. But most of these miserable victims were slaughtered outright, or died in the course of the tortures to which they were subjected.

'The defendants ... are not ignorant men. Most of them are trained physicians and some of them are distinguished scientists. Yet these defendants, all of whom were fully able to comprehend the nature of their acts, and most of whom were exceptionally qualified to form a moral and professional judgment in this respect, are responsible for wholesale murder and unspeakably cruel tortures ...

'The perverse thoughts and distorted concepts which brought these savageries are not dead. They cannot be killed by force of arms. They must not become a spreading cancer in the breast of humanity. They must be cut out and exposed'. 'And he went on to say that it was the duty of the tribunal to ensure – 'that these incredible events be established by clear and public proof; so that no one can ever doubt that they were fact and not fable; and that

---

* The proceedings have not been published in full, but are open to inspection at the Library of Congress, Washington. Extensive selections appear in *Trials of War Criminals before the Nurenberg Military Tribunals under Control Law No. 10* Vols. I and II, *The Medical Case* (abr. M. C.), U.S. Government Printing Office. See also A. Mitscherlich & E. Mielke, *The Death Doctors* (abr. D. D.), Elek Books, 1962. The U.S. Government claims no copyright in this material.

this Court, as the agent of the United States and the voice of humanity, stamp these acts and the ideas which engendered them as barbarous and criminal.' (M.C. I. 27-28)

All this was duly done: the reality of 'these incredible events' was proved, and set down in a record of nearly twelve thousand pages; seven of the accused were hanged, and nine were sentenced to varying terms of imprisonment. But to whom were such events 'incredible'? They were of a kind that had been predicted often enough. They could not have been incredible to anyone conversant with the history of vivisection, nor to anyone who had read the comments made on it by Bernard Shaw in 1900 in *The Dynamitards of Science*, or by Alfred Russel Wallace in 1912 in *The World of Life*. They were incredible only to people who had chosen to be blind.

It is not to be doubted that there were sadists on the staffs of the concentration camps, and perhaps some of the camp-doctors were among them. These persons assisted in the programme of experimentation on prisoners, but it was not by them that it was designed. After a small-scale beginning, the planning of it passed into the hands of the highest medical experts – men such as Professor Rose, Head of the Department of Tropical Medicine at the Robert Koch Institute; Professor Rostock, Head of the Department of Surgery at the University of Berlin; Dr Sievers, Deputy Chairman of the Reich Research Council; Dr Gebhardt, President of the German Red Cross; Professor Brandt and Dr Conti, Commissioners of State for Public Health and Hygiene. There were others, not all of whom were brought to trial.

It would be less disturbing if one could class these people as sadistic monsters and have done with them; but that would be to miss the significance of their behaviour and its implications. These men were not monsters. Some of them were eminent scientists, and most had been able to satisfy their consciences at every step. There is a fearful fascination in seeing how a person who is normal, intelligent, and in many ways humane, may gradually come, in certain of his activities, to behave atrociously. The first step in this type of atrocity is animal-vivisection. The experiments made on prisoners were many and diverse, but they had one thing in common: all were in continuation of, or complementary to experiments on animals. In every instance, this antecedent scientific literature is mentioned in the evidence; and at Buchenwald and Auschwitz concentration camps, human and animal experiments were carried out simultaneously as parts of a single programme.

This unification, which Shaw and others had foreseen, is possible only because man and the higher animals are closely related. We are of one family, however diverse we may appear. And when the repugnance of a normal person to performing painful experiments on animals has been overcome, he has taken the first step towards human vivisection. How does he take the second step? One of the accused at Nuremberg, Dr Ruff, was asked if he had had any qualms when called upon to use camp-prisoners.

'I had no scruples on legal grounds,' he replied, 'for I knew that the man who had officially authorized these experiments was Himmler. He was at that time at the Ministry of the Interior. Consequently, I had no scruples of any kind in that direction. In the sphere of what one may call medical ethics, it was rather different. It was a wholly new experience for us to be offered prisoners to experiment on. Accordingly, both Dr Romberg and myself had to get used to the idea.' (D.D. p. 46–47)

So, if the law permits, the second step is taken in the same manner as the first – by getting used to the idea. And one reason for recalling this trial is to show how easily this can be done, and how thoroughly many of those who did it believed themselves to be justified. 'My life, my actions, and my aims were clean,' Dr Mrugrowski said in his last speech to the Court. 'That is why now, at the end of this trial, I can declare myself free of personal guilt.' He was sentenced to be hanged.

That was a part of the closing scene, and we must now look back to the beginning.

The war-time experiments on prisoners – there had been others before the war – seem to have been first suggested by Dr Rascher, a surgeon in the Luftwaffe. He needed to know what would happen to a pilot, flying at heights that had never been reached before, in various emergencies. It was believed that a parachutist jumping at an altitude of twelve kilometres would suffer severe injuries, and would probably die. But was this correct? For how long could a man live without oxygen above the normal breathing limits? Would he be able to operate life-saving equipment? Rascher required the answer to these and to some other questions quickly; and so he wrote to Himmler, with whom he was on friendly terms. The letter is dated 15 May 1941.

'My most sincere thanks for your cordial wishes and flowers on the birth of my second son. This time, too, it is a strong boy, though he arrived three weeks too early. I shall take the liberty of sending you a small picture of both children some time . [He then explained his research problem and continued] I therefore put the serious question: is there any possibility that two or three professional criminals can be made available for these experiments? ... The experiments, in which the experimental subject of course may die, would take place with my collaboration. They are absolutely essential for the research on high-altitude flying and cannot, as has been tried until now, be carried out on monkeys; because monkeys offer entirely different test conditions.' (M.C. I. 141-42)

Himmler agreed readily. Two or three professional criminals was a modest request. But when the final report was submitted about a year later, over two hundred persons had been used, and seventy or eighty had died. These experiments were carried out at

Air Chief Marshal Lord Dowding

Professor S. T. Aygün

Dachau concentration camp, in a low-pressure chamber in the laboratory. Less than a third were designed to be fatal; but all were painful, and the minute-by-minute record of some of them is one of agony. The findings, however, were of value; and it may have been due to this that senior scientists – men of much higher standing than Dr Rascher – were able to get used to the idea so quickly. Experimentation on prisoners was a method by which other urgent problems might be solved.

The war with Russia raised questions of exposure to cold – both for airmen shot down in the Baltic and for soldiers on the battlefields. How long could a man hope to survive in freezing water? What was the best protective clothing? What are the surest methods of resuscitation? About three hundred people were allocated for these researches, and, once again, not quite a third of them died. Some were immersed for hours in water near to freezing-point, some were exposed naked throughout a winter night. It was found that anaesthetics introduced unnatural conditions, and many of the subjects were therefore conscious. They screamed as parts of their bodies froze. The results, however, were informative and led to a new treatment for exposure. Afterwards, when Germany was invaded by the allies and this treatment was discovered, it was at once adopted by American air-sea rescue services and is probably still in use. Questioned on these supercooling experiments at his trial, Professor Brandt said:

'The most influential factor in deciding whether or not to carry out experiments is the importance of such work. When this factor was considered in relation to the chilling tests proposed, their importance under war conditions was agreed . . . At bottom, the individual did not count any longer.' (D.D. pp. 342)

Brandt had satisfied his own conscience, but he was sentenced to death and hanged. This may be thought to raise an incidental question; for it may seem inconsistent to some people to hang a scientist for discovering a treatment of which one is making use. But it is not necessarily so. Facts are not moral or immoral in themselves. Once they are known, by whatever means they were discovered, one cannot unknow them; and once they have been built into the general structure of knowledge, one cannot avoid putting them to use. The facts of science are inextricably interwoven, and it is impossible to sift out and reject those that were discovered by immoral methods. There was no inconsistency, therefore, in employing the treatment and executing the discoverers.

Conditions on the Russian front led also to the more terrible research on the sulphonomides. Knowledge of these drugs was further advanced in the allied countries; and the Russians had been dropping propaganda leaflets, in which they claimed to possess a miracle-medicine which prevented the infection of wounds. The treatment being given by the German Medical Army Service was out of date, and an urgent investigation into the sulphonomides was called for. It was planned by Professor Gebhardt, President of the German Red Cross, and largely carried out by his assistant, Dr Fischer.

This programme was particularly horrible to implement. The wounds had to be inflicted deliberately, and then infected, before the efficacy of various forms of treatment could be assessed. The preliminaries were done under an anaesthetic. Tetanus, gas gangrene, and oedema malignum were among the infections induced; and the subjects were then divided into groups and treated by different methods. The victims selected for these tests were inmates of the Ravensbrück concentration camp for women; and one of the survivors, scarred and crippled, gave evidence at Nuremberg. She said she had been taken to the operating theatre of the camp-hospital on the fourteenth of August, 1942. She did not know why. Several surgeons were present, who were evidently preparing to perform an operation. No one spoke to her, and she was given an intravenous injection:

'I regained consciousness in the morning, and then I noticed that my leg was in a cast from the ankle up to the knee, and I felt a very great pain in this leg and had a high temperature ... The pain was increasing and the temperature too, and the next day I noticed that some liquid was flowing from my leg. The third day I was put on a hospital trolley and taken to the dressing-room ... A blanket was put over my eyes and I did not know what was done with my leg, but I felt great pain and I had the impression that something must have been cut out ... Three days later I was again taken to the dressing-room, and the dressing was changed by Dr Fischer with the assistance of the same doctors, and I was also blindfolded. I was then sent back to the regular hospital ward ... Two weeks later we were all taken to the operating theatre again, and put on the operating tables. The bandage was removed, and that was the first time I saw my leg. The incision went so deep that I could see the bone.' (M.C. I. 412-13)

At his trial, Dr Fischer said: 'I had never previously thought in any practical way about experiments on human beings. I knew, however, that in the history of medicine such experiments had been carried out; but I never studied such things, and it was my resolve and my wish not to have anything to do with such a question or the problems it involved ... I regret that fate compelled me to transgress as a doctor the fundamental principle of *nihil nocere*. I also regret that people have come forward to bear witness that I did not help, but rather inflicted injuries on them. I am particularly sorry that they should have been women. But ... my own basic motive for the conduct that has brought me before this court was solely my desire to help the wounded.'* And he went on to explain that Professor Gebhardt, in whom he had complete confidence, had assured him that these experiments were necessary. Gebhardt corroborated all this and added one point: 'During

---

* D.D. pp. 186-92.

the entire period in question, I had experiments in my field of research carried out on animals.'*

Many eminent people had by that time accepted human vivisection. A report on the Ravensbrück experiments, read by Dr Fischer and introduced by Professor Gebhardt, was made to a meeting of consultant specialists in May 1943. Some two hundred were present. They were told that the subjects had been under sentence of death. In the discussion that followed, no questions were asked on this aspect of the matter: reluctantly, tacitly, but decisively, the Army Medical Academy had conceded the principle. But this did not save the defendants at Nuremberg. Dr Fischer was sentenced to life-imprisonment, and Professor Gebhardt to death.

By 1943 the experimental programme had progressed a long way beyond the 'two or three professional criminals' whom Dr Rascher had tentatively requested in 1941. A few had grown to thousands. Each successive step had been taken logically; and from the scientific point of view the programme could hardly be faulted. The men who planned it were not sadists; most of them had succeeded in satisfying rather than stifling their consciences. And they undoubtedly desired to help the wounded. The wounded had many different needs. Bone-grafting for shattered limbs was one of them. Once again, the unfortunate women-prisoners at Ravensbrück were selected for these investigations. Their bones were broken, transplanted, grafted, in an experimental series that seems to become increasingly diabolical. Then typhus broke out on the Russian front, and a new research centre was set up – this time at Buchenwald.

Professor Rose, Chief of the Department of Tropical Medicine at the Robert Koch Institute, made an eloquent defence of these experiments. In the course of his trial, he said:

'Dr Conti, Chief of the Medical Service, was called upon to

* M.C. II, 145.

decide whether he should allow mass production and utilization of an unknown vaccine or ... seek state sanction for experiments on human beings, in order to determine the efficacy of the vaccines proposed. Conti decided on the latter alternative, which involved risking and in some cases sacrificing the lives of a number of duly nominated persons ... If it had not been for the Buchenwald experiments, the vaccines which they proved unserviceable would have been put into mass production; for they were all much easier and cheaper to manufacture than the serviceable vaccines ... We know today how many of the subjects of experiment perished; but we cannot, naturally, prove how many lives were saved.' (D.D. 144-46)

It was the best defence that could have been offered; but Professor Rose, unlike some of his colleagues, had always had misgivings; and he cannot have listened unmoved to the evidence of a prosecution witness who described conditions in the special block at Buchenwald where the typhus experiments were carried out:

'Every man in the camp knew that Block 46 was a dreadful place. Only a very few people had an exact idea of what was going on in Block 46. A dreadful horror seized anyone who was brought into any kind of connection with this block. If people were selected and taken to Block 46 through the sick bay, then they knew that the affair was a fatal one. The untold horror that attached to this block made things even worse ... In this mental condition the experimental persons waited in the sick bays for an unknown period of time. They waited for the day or for the night when something would be done to them; they did not know what it would be, but they guessed it would be some frightful form of death. If they were vaccinated, sometimes the most terrible scenes took place, because the patients were afraid the injections were lethal ... When the actual illness had set in after the infection, ordinary symptoms of typhus would appear. The infection, as I have already described to you, became so powerful during the last two and a half years that the typhus almost always appeared in its most horrible form. There were cases of raving madness, delirium, people would refuse to eat, and a large percentage of them would die. Those who experienced the disease in a milder form were forced continually to observe the death-struggles of the others. All this took place in an atmosphere hardly possible to imagine.' (M.C. I. 585)

While this was happening in Block 46, complimentary experiments were being made on animals in Block 50. Dr Conti hanged himself, and Professor Rose was sentenced to imprisonment for life.

Up to this point, the research had at least been concerned with actual and urgent problems. This did not continue to be the case. It progressed to hypothetical questions, then to pure science, and finally to something that borders on science-fiction. The first hypothetical question arose from the possibility that chemical weapons might be used. In fact they were not, but the question remained: if there were gas-attacks and mass-casualties resulted, what would be the best treatment? Experiments to determine this with regard to mustard-gas and phosgene began at Natzweiler concentration camp in the autumn of 1942. The Chief Orderly at the camp-hospital there was a prosecution witness at Nuremberg, and he described the mustard-gas experiments.

'In the middle of October, certain prisoners who were still to some extent fit, that is, still looked fairly healthy, were selected by Professor Hirt and taken to two rooms, into each of which fifteen men were introduced. They were at first, for about fourteen days, put on SS diet. Then the experiments began . . . The prisoners were stripped quite naked. They came into the laboratory one by one. There I was told to hold their arms, while they were given one drop of the liquid 10 cms above the forearm. Then they had to go into the next room and stand for about an hour with their arms spread out. Some ten hours later, or perhaps after a rather longer interval, the burns made their appearance, covering the whole body. The body was scorched wherever the gas exhalatations reached it. Some of the subjects were blinded. They suffered intense pain, so that one could hardly bear to be near them. The first fatalities occurred on about the fifth or sixth day ... The intestines, lungs, and so on were found to be eaten away. During the next few days another seven people died. Treatment lasted about two months. Then those who were still to some extent capable of travelling were dispatched to another camp.' (D.D. 217)

An emotional defence was offered for this – concern for women and children; it is needless to quote it here. But what is now evident is that the first small rivulet had become a flood. This accords with the history of animal-experiments, which have grown from a few hundreds annually to uncounted millions. Scientists have been demoralized by the acceptance of the principle that the power confers the right. As a result, it is now scarcely an exaggeration to say that to think of a biological problem is to think of an experimental animal. And for the most important biological problems, the most suitable animal is man.

The end in view may be beneficent, but it is not always so. There are problems of destruction as well as preservation. The poison-gas experiments were poised between. This research was still inspired by therapeutic motives; but moral restraints had been so weakened that further research could not resist a corrupt motive, and what follows seems like the realization of a sadistic phantasy. That is perhaps what it was, for the problem itself had become malevolent. How, short of actual massacre, could unwanted elements in the population, mainly but not only Jewish, be removed.

The least-objectionable answer was mass-sterilization, which would have disposed of the problem within a generation; but the numbers involved were too great for this to be practicable by normal methods. The alternative proposed was mass-castration by means of X-rays, and it was suggested that this might be done without the subjects' knowledge. They might be required, for example, to stand at a special counter while filling in a lengthy form; and during this time, although unaware of it, they would be subjected to radiation of sufficient intensity to castrate them. It was hoped that large numbers of men and women could be expeditiously treated in this way, and experiments on its feasibility were carried out at Auswitz in 1943. At that stage of the project, however, the experimental subjects, some of whom were children, were agonizingly aware of the research that was being done on them. The full story, or nearly all of it, was told in the courtroom at Nuremberg; but it is too horrible to be recounted in this book.

When so much had been conceded, the demands of pure knowledge could hardly be denied. There will always be some people who believe that the advancement of science is of paramount importance, and who will claim, like Professor Slosson, that 'a human life is nothing compared with a new fact.' They are likely to be people who have partly identified themselves with science, and who are using it unconsciously for their own self-inflation. Only the law can check them. Such a man, one is driven to suppose, was Dr August Hirt, Professor of Anatomy at the University of Strasbourg. On the ninth of February 1942, he wrote a Memorandum, to be submitted by intermediaries to Himmler, which is among the most bizarre documents in the literature of science.

'There exist,' he wrote, 'extensive collections of skulls of almost all races and peoples. Of the Jewish race, however, only so very few specimens of skulls are at the disposal of science that a study of them does not permit precise conclusions. The war in the East now presents us with the opportunity to remedy this shortage. By procuring the skulls of the Jewish Bolshevik Commissars, who personify a repulsive yet characteristic subhumanity, we have the opportunity of obtaining tangible scientific evidence. The actual obtaining and collecting of these skulls could best be accomplished by a directive issued to the Wehrmacht to turn over alive all Jewish Bolshevik Commissars to the field police. The field police, in turn, is to be issued special directives to inform a certain office of the number and place of detention of these captured Jews, and to guard them well until the arrival of a special deputy. This special deputy . . . is to take a prescribed series of photographs and anthropological measurements, and is to ascertain the origin, date of birth, and other personal data of the prisoner. Following the subsequently induced death of the Jew, whose head must not be damaged, he will separate the head from the torso, and will forward it to its point of destination in a well sealed tin container especially made for this purpose.' (M.C. I. 739)

Professor Hirt then suggested that the Anatomical Institute at Strasbourg would be the best place for the subsequent research. Himmler agreed to this in principle; but it was decided to procure the skulls, not from the battlefield, but a concentration camp. An epidemic interrupted the collecting until the summer of 1943, and the Professor's plans had then become more ambitious. Skulls no longer sufficed: his new programme necessitated complete bodies, and it required them to be still warm. A special gas-chamber was constructed at Natzweiler to supply him with corpses in the specified state. It was ready at the end of July. At his trial, Joseph Kramer, Commandant at Natzweiler, described the occasion of its first use:

'At the beginning of August 1943, I received the eighty inmates who were to be gassed with the stuff Hirt had handed me. One evening about nine o'clock, I went to the gas-chamber in a small van with about fifteen women for a start. I told them they would have to go to the disinfection room, but I did not tell them they were to be poisoned. With the help of some SS. men I stripped them completely, and when they were quite naked pushed them into the gas-chamber. As soon as the door was shut they began screaming ... I turned on the interior light ... and looked through the peep-hole to see what was happening in the room. I observed that the women went on breathing for about half-a-minute before they fell down. I switched on the flue-ventilation and then opened the doors. The women were all lying dead on the floor ... Next morning at about 5.30, I told the SS. hospital orderlies to load the corpses into a small van, so that they could be taken to the Anatomical Institute as Professor Hirt had instructed.' (D.D. 226)

The account is completed by the employee at the Institute who met the van:

'The preservation process began at once. The bodies were still warm when they arrived. Their eyes were wide open and glazing. The eyeballs were bloodshot, red and protuberant. There were also traces of blood about the noses and mouths. The discharge of other liquids was perceptible in some cases. There was no sign of rigor mortis ... A few days later we received a second consignment, consisting of thirty men, in exactly the same condition as the first, still warm ... The preservation of these thirty male corpses was immediately undertaken in the same way, except for one small detail. In each case the left testicle was removed and sent to the Anatomical Laboratory, which was that of Professor Hirt himself.' (D.D. 227-28)

When the course of the war brought Strasbourg into the danger zone, some apprehension was felt that this collection might be found by the allies and its purpose be misunderstood. At Hirt's request, therefore, Wolfram Sievers wrote to Himmler for instructions:

'Professor Dr Hirt has assembled a skeleton collection which has never been in existence before. Because of the vast amount of scientific research that is connected with this project, the work of reducing the corpses to skeletons has not yet been completed. Since it might require some time to process eighty corpses, Hirt requested a decision pertaining to the treatment of the collection stored in the morgue of the Anatomy, in case Strasbourg should be endangered. The collection can be defleshed and rendered unrecognizable. This, however, would mean that the work had been done for nothing – at least in part – and this singular collection would be lost to science.' (D.D. 229)

The reply was an order that the collection should be destroyed; but this was not completely done, and part of it fell into the hands of the French.

When the war ended, Professor Hirt had disappeared. He was presumed to be dead. But if he had lived, and had been brought to trial, he would certainly have found something to say in his own defence. 'These researches', he would have claimed, 'were of value to science.' No doubt they were, but this is science run amok. And it is important for a society that has exempted the pursuit of knowledge from the laws against cruelty to know that this can happen, and that enquiries that employ such methods may end in the nightmare of a mad professor.

The prosecution at Nuremberg spoke of these events as 'incredible', but we have no right to find them so. People better-known that Frances Cobbe had, in a general sense, foretold them. 'It will land you in horrors of which you have no conception,' had been the prophecy of Bernard Shaw. The reality may have exceeded his expectations, but it was in line with them. And it should not be incredible to us, who are still sowing a cruel seed, if we reap a cruel harvest.

CHAPTER SIXTEEN

A New Vision of Life

On the eighteenth of June 1940, after the fall of France, Winston Churchill made one of his great speeches in the House of Commons, and he ended with the words:

'What General Weygand called the Battle of France is over. I expect that the Battle of Britain is about to begin. Upon this battle depends the survival of Christian civilization. Upon it depends our own British life, and the long continuity of our institutions and our Empire. The whole fury and might of the enemy must very soon be turned on us. Hitler knows that he will have to break us in this island or lose the war. If we can stand up to him, all Europe may be free and the life of the world may move forward into broad, sunlit uplands. But if we fail, then the whole world, including the United States, including all we have known and cared for, will sink into the abyss of a new Dark Age, made more sinister, and perhaps more protracted, by the lights of perverted science. Let us therefore brace ourselves to our duties, and so bear ourselves that, if the British Empire and its Commonwealth last for a thousand years, men will still say: "This was their finest hour." '*

During the three months that followed, the multitudes of Europe were almost helpless lookers-on while the future was determined in the skies between the fighter planes of the Royal Air Force and the bombers of the Luftwaffe. Immense land and sea forces were all-but immobile pending the outcome; and Hitler as well as Churchill believed it would decide the course of history

* Hansard, June 18th, 1940.

for the next thousand years. This was the first and only air conflict that ranks among the decisive battles of the world.

The Air Officer Commanding in Chief Fighter Command during the Battle of Britain, as everyone knows, was Air Chief Marshal Sir Hugh Dowding. Had it not been for his genius, the battle might have been lost; and but for his foresight, it might not have been fought. The aircraft needed to fight it would have been lost on the other side of the Channel, during the Battle of France, if he had not intervened with the War Cabinet; and the system of underground control centres, which was no less indispensable to victory than the Hurricanes and the Spitfires, was the creation of his inspired planning in the years before the war. There is no one man to whom the western world is more indebted for its liberty.

In 1943, Dowding was raised to the peerage; and this gave him the opportunity to speak when he wished to do so in the House of Lords. He did not often exercise this right; but among his infrequent speeches there were several against cruelty. And after his retirement, it was in this battle that he chiefly served. It is still very far from being won. But until it has been won, the threat of 'a new Dark Age, made more sinister by the lights of perverted science', will remain; and the world will not, as Churchill hoped, 'move forward into broad, sunlit uplands'. Indeed, it may well regress; for there is nothing that so darkens and devalues life as cruelty.

It was twelve years after the Battle of Britain, on the fourteenth of October 1952, that Dowding first addressed the House of Lords on the subject of vivisection. The wider background of this speech was a world rebuilding its shattered cities, redesigning its society, awakened by suffering to the need of a new ethic and new values, and in which stupendous progress in the science of destruction had made peace almost a condition of man's existence. What it needed, and what this speech proposed, was a new vision of life:

'My Lords, I am speaking today on an unpopular subject. People who are normally humane have the idea that the suffering inflicted on animals by surgical and medical experiments avails to reduce the suffering of human beings. I want to make clear at the outset my own personal position. It is this: that even should it be conclusively proved that human beings benefit directly from the suffering of animals, its infliction would nevertheless be unethical and wrong . . . I am sure that the average man and woman in this country has not yet learnt to appreciate the part played by animals in the great drama of evolution, or our responsibilities towards animals, or the ill-effects which follow our neglect of those responsibilities.'

After pointing out some defects in the law which we need not recapitulate, he continued:

'The process of preparing this motion has been a most painful one to me, because it has compelled me to read of many cases of revolting and sickening cruelty. I do not wish to base my appeal to your Lordships on sentimentality, or to attempt to work up a reaction beyond that which is justified by the facts. But this is a subject that is resolutely thrust aside by the average citizen, by the Press, and the broadcasting authorities – in which I include the Church. They wish to believe that all is well with the existing system, and that its only critics are cranks. They have no wish even to listen to the evidence, and so my case would not be complete if I did not adduce some instances in support of my assertions.'

Readers of this book will not require further instances, and it is Dowding's personal contribution to the subject that is of interest at this point. He wished to convince his hearers that to face and to remedy these abuses is an indispensable condition of the better world that we are attempting to build; and that we, as a nation, still have an opportunity to lead, to serve, and to be great:

'The time has gone, perhaps never to return, when Britain could mould the world to her will by force of arms or by the power of money. But I am one of those who believe that the power of Britain will be exercised, and effectively exercised, through the example we set to other nations of humanity in the widest sense of the word.'*

No grander aim has ever been proposed to Parliament; and no one could have had a better title to propose it than the man to whom the nation already owed so much – its freedom and the attainment of its finest hour. To all those who were listening to this speech, that was a recent memory; but the majority heard it with indifference, and their answer was rejection. There were some who understood that he was not pleading for tormented animals only, but for the dignity of man and his right to happiness. But it is a measure, perhaps, of the extent to which the dark side of science has clouded the human spirit that so few were able to recognize that its cruelties are a malignant sickness, one that will spread, as it spread to the concentration camps, until it has infected not only our relationship with the simpler animals but also with our fellow human beings, and, whether there is a God or not, until it has destroyed the sense and concept of the divine in life. It touches the quality and therefore the value of our existence. And when we have spoken grandiloquently of all that we are supposed to be, and might be, then perhaps we shall consider what we are in danger of becoming – the scourge of nature and the 'universal wolf'.

Five years later, on the eighteenth of July 1957, Dowding spoke in the House of Lords again. He gave fresh instances and drew attention to the secrecy in which vivisection is practised – 'behind the closed doors of laboratories to which the public has no access.' And at the end of his speech, he carried the argument for the necessity of a new ethic, which, as we have seen, has been gathering strength in modern Europe since at least the time of Victor Hugo, a stage further:

'All life is one, and all its manifestations with which we have

* Hansard, October 14th, 1952.

contact are climbing the ladder of evolution. The animals are our younger brothers and sisters, also on the ladder, but a few rungs lower down than we are. It is an important part of our responsibilities to help them in their ascent, and not to retard their development by cruel exploitation of their helplessness. What I am now saying, if people would realize it, is of very great practical importance, because failure to recognize our responsibilities towards the animal kingdom is the cause of many of the calamities which now beset the nations of the world. Nearly all of us have a deep-rooted wish for peace, peace on earth; but we shall never attain to true peace – the peace of love, and not the uneasy equilibrium of fear – until we recognize the place of the animals in the scheme of things and treat them accordingly.'*

What we need, in fact, is a new way of life founded on compassion for all living things; and that this should have been said in the House of Lords, by the commander of 'the few' who won the Battle of Britain, is among the significant events of the post-war years, and a portent, one may believe, of the greater victory.

Some of Lord Dowding's hearers may have thought this part of his speech to be visionary, and they may have been right; but that was not a good reason for its dismissal. A race that has invented the means of its own destruction, and that lives under their shadow, is in dire need of vision; and nothing less than the unity of life, and the ethic that derives from it, can reconcile scientific with spiritual values, reason with love. If man on earth is to have a future, this must be done; for there is no other guarantee against a misuse of power by which we ourselves should be destroyed.

Only one peer, Lord Somers, gave Lord Dowding his support. The Lords Spiritual, if any were present, said nothing; the field was left to the Scientific Lords. It was in consequence of this rebuff that Dowding requested an interview with the Home Secretary. The encounter was illuminating, and has been referred to already

* Hansard, July 18th, 1957.

in this book: he was informed that the government would not lift a finger to interfere with vivisection as long as its advisers considered that it was necessary. A Home Secretary, of course, can speak only for the government in office; but as history shows this attitude to be a constant, it raises the question, previously discussed, by whom are governments advised? The answer supplies the reason why every attempt – and there have been many – to amend this Act in a humane manner has been blocked for a hundred years.

These speeches, however, were not entirely fruitless; and pressure was being brought to bear on the government from other quarters. In 1961, the Royal Society for the Prevention of Cruelty to Animals sent a deputation to the Home Secretary, which pressed for a number of reforms, including representation of animal-welfare societies on the Advisory Committee. In face of this mounting offensive, the government was driven to concede an enquiry; and in May 1963 – almost eleven years after Lord Dowding's first motion in the House of Lords – a Departmental Committee was appointed, under the chairmanship of Sir Sydney Littlewood, which was charged: 'To consider the present control over experiments on living animals, and to consider whether, and if so what, changes are desirable in the law or its administration.'

This must be accounted a battle won, but not a notable victory: the report of the Committee was presented to Parliament in 1965, and ever since it has been left to gather dust.

* * *

The Report of the Littlewood Committee will not be analysed here; but it differs in one respect from previous enquiries into the subject, and this invites reflection. To be quite without prejudice is impossible. This is not a question of integrity, but of human nature. The least prejudiced person, perhaps, is one who knows what his prejudices are; but the majority of people are scarcely aware of them. It follows that a committee that has to consider a problem, especially if it is a social or a moral problem, cannot do so without bias – the resultant, as it were, of the individual tendencies to bias among its members. This is inevitable, not discreditable; but the authority appointing a committee might conceivably take advantage of this fact by selecting persons to serve on it whose outlook was sympathetic to the policies it desired to pursue. There are times when this must be a temptation. It was for these reasons that Lord Truro, speaking of the first official enquiry into experimentation on animals, once reminded the House of Lords that even a Royal Commission cannot be entirely impartial.*

The two Royal Commissions on vivisection, however, provided a corrective to their partiality. They published the full verbatim evidence from which their conclusions had been drawn. The facts and opinions that had been laid before them were all made known to the public, and anyone who chose to read these could judge the matter for himself. In consequence, their Reports and Minutes of Evidence were not only a fine presentation of the state of affairs at the time, but they have ever since remained historical documents of great value.

Such a full public statement of the facts, which are otherwise notoriously difficult to come by, was greatly needed when the Littlewood Committee was set up. The Committee had before it the precedent of two exemplary publications, but it did not follow this. It published no Minutes, and it produced a Report that does not contain one sentence of verbatim evidence. All the evidence it offers is paraphrased, and much of it is anonymous. No jury would accept it. And the reader of this Report is not placed in a position to form an independent judgment.

The effect of a paraphrase is to accentuate a bias. And if it is impossible for any group of people to be without some collective prejudice, then it is pertinent to ask what the prejudices of the

* See Hansard's Parliamentary Debates, July 15, 1879.

Littlewood Committee were. Not everyone will agree on the answer, which is clearly not easy to assess; but in the opinion of the present writer, the Committee was influenced by at least two unconscious motives – to reassure the public, and to refrain from interfering with vivisection.

As we do not know what the evidence was, we cannot gauge the accuracy of the paraphrase. There is, however, one instance that constitutes an exception. The Royal Society for the Prevention of Cruelty to Animals did, of course, give evidence. The Society has an official policy on vivisection, which it claims to have made plain to the Committee, and it is this:

'The Society's attitude towards experiments on animals remains the same today as from the outset, namely that it opposes all experiments that cause pain or suffering.'

In the Report, this appears as follows: 'The general policy of the Society was not to oppose experiments on animals even where these caused pain.' That is a complete misrepresentation. Of course, it was not intentional; but it remains a revealing error. It is evidence of a certain carelessness; it shows how unreliable a paraphrase can be; and it indicates, perhaps, what the Committee would have liked to believe, and in what sense its bias lay. There are some other passages that abide our question, and the unpublished Minutes of Evidence exist. But anyone who is anxious to pry into them will doubtless receive the same answer as was given to the present writer: 'I am not permitted to divulge their contents.'

This is not the kind of enquiry for which the humane movement had been asking. The doors are still closed.

CHAPTER SEVENTEEN

The World Problem and the Grounds of Protest

It is important to recognize that this is an international problem, and that it cannot be dealt with by national societies alone. Just as the findings of science are world possessions, so cruelty in research is a world reproach. In the scientific sense, it is usually of slight importance in which country a particular discovery is made; and in the humanitarian sense, it is of no importance whatever on which side of a frontier some creature suffers. To grapple with this evil requires an international outlook, and a grouping of societies that will make the anti-vivisection movement into a world-force. As we have seen, splendid efforts to do this have been exerted in the past; but the two great wars, and dissension between societies, have so far frustrated them. A new attempt is now being made to build an effective international organization.* Will it succeed? The answer must largely depend on whether the lessons of a hundred years of anti-vivisection history have been thoroughly learnt, and on whether it will prove possible, at last, to combine realistic statesmanship with the ideal aim. The need is urgent; and it should now be plain to all societies, as it is plain to all historians, that leaders who are in conflict with their allies cannot defeat their enemies.

It is impossible to present the world-picture in this book, but some reference must be made to the situation in the United States.

* The International Association against Painful Experiments on Animals, Headquarters: 51 Harley Street, London, W.1.

The United States, especially in the field of science, is now looked on as an example to be copied by many other countries; and for this reason alone, it has a unique importance and bears a unique responsibility. No thorough discussion of vivisection in America will be attempted here, as the magnitude of the problem is far too great. A few figures, relating to the 1960s, will make this evident. During that decade, approximately a thousand million dollars a year of the tax-payers' money was allocated by the Federal Government to biomedical research, and most of this involved the experimental use of animals; some two hundred thousand people were engaged in this work as a full-time activity; more than three hundred million laboratory animals were currently in use, and ten died every second.

There is no equivalent to the British Act in America. Animals undergoing experimentation have no legal protection there, and their plight is consequently much worse; because, as has been stressed already, there is no power except the law that can protect any helpless creature from those who have an interest in its misuse. The British Act is inadequate, but it is not valueless; and its relative worth may be assessed by the difference in the lot of laboratory animals in the two countries. There is a vast difference. This is not due to any contrast in national character; dispositions to kindness or to cruelty are the same on both sides of the Atlantic. The difference is due solely to the fact that on one side there is some law, and on the other there is none. Laws are not merely prohibitive, they are also educative, and those that tend towards justice and mercy serve to establish these values in the public mind. If a law similar to the British had been passed in America in 1876, it is reasonable to believe that the present disparity in the lot of experimental animals would not exist; and the amount of suffering that would have been spared by that, in nearly a hundred years, is beyond imagining.

There have, of course, been many attempts to obtain some law in America. This is a complicated question; because the field of federal legislation is limited by the constitution, and Congress cannot impose anti-cruelty laws on the states. That is a matter for state-legislation. Experimentation on animals, however, is now on so vast a scale that it does involve inter-state transactions in which Congress might intervene. This is debatable for some; but for one, at least, it is unquestionable. As has been said, about a thousand million dollars a year of public money is made available by the Federal Government for biomedical research, and it has an undisputed right – one would have thought a duty – to impose conditions on how this shall be spent. In this field, Congress could prohibit cruelty; and if it did so, the influence of its example on state-legislation would be great.

To this end, numerous Bills have been proposed which have a general resemblance to the British Act; but by the united opposition of those who benefit from this lavish distribution of public funds, all of them have so far been crushed. These interested parties are said to constitute one of the strongest lobbies in Washington. Unfortunately, and this is a further reason for their failure, the anti-vivisection movement in America, as in other countries, is divided on the question of tactics; and the great perfectionist societies are still reluctant to admit the necessity of a gradual approach. It need hardly be said that the whole world movement will neither rest nor give in until painful experiments on animals have been everywhere prohibited by law, and inevitably these Bills did not have that final character. But there has to be reduction before there can be abolition; and faced with the situation as it is now there is only one realistic policy to pursue – to work for the best laws that are obtainable today, and to make them the foundation of the perfect law of tomorrow. Laws are provisional, they are made to be amended and improved; but until there is some legal foundation, there is nothing to amend, nothing to improve, and nothing can be built.

The policy of gradualism also permits the movement to widen its appeal, and so to gain the numerical support that is needed for success. Many people are prepared to go part of the way, but not all the way. At present, however, this is only an academic question. The situation we are confronted with today is so tragic and so pitiful that no ordinary person who knows the facts can believe that it is right. The invitation of the anti-vivisection movement should therefore be to everybody: 'Come with us as far as you wish to come, and leave us when your own conscience is satisfied. We need your help *now* to end the most flagrant abuses, and we may leave it to another generation to argue over fine distinctions.'

This book is not intended to be an anthology of horror, although that would have been easy to compile. Its readers have not been harrowed more than the subject demands; but in writing the story of a reform movement, it is necessary to exhibit its grounds. And lest these should still seem insufficient, some evidence must be given in its final pages. Many will find this distressing, but it is hoped that they will read it thoughtfully and make it known; because until these things are known, they will not be remedied, and until they have been remedied, the human race has no right to happiness.

The evidence is vast and overwhelming, but it does not reach the public. There is a barrier of silence to be broken through. The primary records are written in technical language which is in itself forbidding, and the information supplied by the humane societies is mostly in leaflets that are soon lost. Occasionally, there are official publications of great value; but these, too, are quickly forgotten and left to gather dust. They retain the advantages of easy reference, however, and of a standing that cannot be surpassed. For these reasons, the extracts that follow are all taken from one official source, published by the United States Government. This publication is the minutes of evidence laid before a sub-committee of the House of Representatives in September, 1962. These hearings were in connection with two Bills, which had some resemblance to the British Act; the Bills failed to pass, but the enquiry was of great value. The text is long – three hundred and seventy-five pages, many in close print. Thirty-three witnesses appeared in person, and a number of others sent statements that were filed. The evidence is not paraphrased: it is what each witness said. Only a few extracts can be quoted here, but it is hoped that they will serve as brief glimpses through windows that are usually shuttered to the public view. We cannot stand and stare.

The selected quotations refer mainly to dogs, because brevity is imperative in this book; but it should be remembered that a wide variety of species suffer, and are mentioned in the record. I would ask members of the great perfectionist societies, when they study this evidence, carefully to consider whether it does not prove two things – that to remedy everything at once is an impossibility, and that to remedy nothing is a tragedy. And I would also beg those distinguished men, who have written and spoken for the various Research Defence Societies, to read the full official record and reflect that this – and immeasurable more and worse than this – is what they are committed to defend.

* * *

Humane Treatment of Animals Used in Research: Hearings before a Subcommittee of the Committee on Interstate and Foreign Commerce, House of Representatives, on H.R. 1937 and H.R. 3556, September 28 and 29, 1962. For sale by the Superintendent of Documents, U.S. Government Printing Office, Washington, D.C.

The following quotations are taken from the testimony of many different people, most of whom were eye-witnesses, and all of whom are named. Their evidence relates to numerous establishments – some appertaining to the government, some to universities, and some to industry – and it comes from all quarters of the United States. These details have been omitted here, but they may easily be found in the record; and for the convenience of those who wish to study the complete text—and it is hoped that many will – the page-reference is given before each excerpt.

222 'The conditions under which animals are being used in research constitutes the most intense and shameful of all the nation-wide cruelties to animals.'

119 'In those windowless, sub-basement rooms, hundreds of dogs flung themselves against the bars of their cages piled tier on tier. They were barking, screaming, whining. A few were mute – and drooped their heads in the dark corners. Others circled ceaselessly in their cages ... These dogs, mostly beagles, are used primarily for testing food additives. Some remain in their cages for seven years. We often refer to places we love as a little bit of heaven. Each of these rooms is a little bit of hell ... I was appalled when Food and Drug Administration scientists told me that when they obtained a new twenty-six million dollar office and laboratory building, they planned to continue lifetime caging of these hundreds of dogs.'

271 'In many animal-rooms, the cages are stacked in tiers, so that it is impossible to clean them properly. Often on a Sunday no one is in attendance, so no animal gets any fresh water or food.'

252 'The cages in which these dogs are kept have wire bottoms – heavy chicken wire. I found one dog imprisoned for two days, the animal-boys said with his long toe-nails caught in the wire, people knowing of it and doing nothing. A puppy there had finally chewed his foot off to free it from the wire.'

76 'These quarters are new ... so the decision to house dogs in basement cages three tiers high, without provision for exercise, and to hose the cages with the dogs inside them was deliberate.

'Most pitiful were those whose painful and debilitating surgery prevented them from rising, and who were soaking and shivering in the bottoms of the wet cages, from which they would never be taken again unless it were for further experimentation or as carcasses.'

83 'All dogs caged, never released for exercise. Three emaciated dogs curled up and uninterested even though most of the dogs were barking furiously. A grey poodle with incredibly matted fur, with food and filth stuck to it ... did not respond in any way, but stood mute and motionless in its cage. A black and tan mongrel was too tall to hold its head up normally. When standing the dog's back was rubbing against the top of the cage. The university refused to build cages any bigger despite urgent requests ... Post-operative room: many were too sick to rise, and some had had two operations. One heart surgical case was emaciated, had a tremor, and lacked one eye from which red flesh extruded ... apparently this did not deter its use for heart surgery ... No attendants in any of the rooms ... none of the dogs we saw had been given any sedation.'

349 'One very sick dog had traces of recent surgery on his right side. I stopped and spoke to the dog, and he made an effort to get up in response. As he did so, large quantities of a bloody, puslike substance exuded from his nostrils and he coughed so hard that he was not able to stand. I called the pathologist's attention to the dog, and asked if something could be done to help him. The pathologist did not know what had been done to the dog (there was no identification of any kind on the cage) and he called the caretaker. The caretaker informed us the dog had had three operations – all unrelated – the last one having been performed six days prior to our visit. I then asked if the dog had received any post-operative care. The pathologist did not know what post-operative care the dog had received – nor did the caretaker. Nothing was done to help this pitiful animal while I was there.'

264 'There is no check whatever upon the wasteful repetition of experiments for which the taxpayer pays; no check on careless planning; no check on the outright sadist, who surrounds his real subconscious motive with a fog of scientific terms.'

218 'In any class of medical students you can always spot a certain number with sadistic tendencies ... medicine provides an opportunity to express these tendencies.'

84 'One medical school dean assured me that cruel people "could get off in a corner and do it anyway." He seemed to take the side of these sadistic characters when he spoke about pending legislation, and with apparent relish remarked, "If I wanted to, I could hide everything away and fool the inspector through the whole medical center." One wonders what he felt needed hiding in this institution which last year received 22 million dollars from the U.S. Public Health Service.'

76 'There is an enormous variety of ways in which they can be made to suffer and die in a laboratory.'

79 'The privilege which our civilization has extended to scientists is being abused.'

59 'I think all of us agree that we need something to combat the influences that are making sadists out of a good many of our young people.'

251 'I am a student studying veterinary medicine. I was never and am not now in the employ of any humane society ... This is a cry and a plea from a young person still holding on to a few ideals I have grown up to believe in – and I am beginning to wonder if there is any real humane goodness among humans. I am not a sentimentalist, a crusader, or a fanatic; but I cannot, under any code or way of human life, condone what I, in a few short years, have seen.'

346 'I attended Chicago Medical School last September. I withdrew of my own accord ... One of the conditions which led to my contempt towards this school was the cruel treatment which was given to the experimental animals.'

250 'Trying to produce convulsions in dogs is terrible. I know they wouldn't let you see that, though. Shock experiments, removal of organs, blocking intestines, or the urine outlet so the bladder ruptures are only run of the mill ... you'd be surprised to hear what professors and some students can think up.

'At night I keep thinking about the dogs. Sometimes I have to walk away, I feel so sick about the dogs.

'Imagine, after you have major surgery and you are between life and death ... your little square of cold, draughty, cement flooring is cleaned by having a hose of cold water squirted over you. The dogs are soaked by this cold water – dogs right after recovering from surgery. No wonder most of the dogs die. But no one cares. If they live, within a couple of days or a week, they are used for a different experiment. One dog survived seven experiments.'

85 'Men who wish to indoctrinate untrained youths into useless pain-infliction cannot be expected to be concerned about unplanned and improperly conducted experiments.

'I have seen dogs in medical schools upon which a series of major operations have been done, pitiful, cringing, emaciated creatures ... They do a series of operations, such as opening the stomach, removing the spleen, removing parts of the intestine and joining it together again, routine castration and speying, and other operations. The dogs become thin and pitiful looking ... they receive no treatment, because they are going to die anyway.'

224 'At Columbia University as many as a thousand blows on each leg of dogs were administered by a rawhide mallet to induce shock. Nervous depression, gasping, thirst and vomiting——not to mention the agonizing pain of crushed muscles, nerves and bones – were some of the effects of the beatings. The researcher who performed this experiment stated that three dogs which survived shock resulting from the beating suddenly expired the following day when they were again placed on the animal-board.'

225 'A *Symposium on Burns* [National Research Council, November, 1950] describes some of the variety of ways in which animals are burned: by gasoline, flame-throwers, burning irons, and for internal burns, hot dry air and steam... A researcher who has burned dogs by means of burning irons held to their shaved skins for one minute, reported in the aforementioned *Symposium on Burns* that "we began a study on a series of dogs that were irradiated with 100 per cent total body irradiation, in addition to twenty per cent body-surface burn ... we do not know of any practical method of irradiating these dogs and burning them at the same time in the laboratory, which is a goal we would like to achieve.'

85 'In short, the view of the National Society for Medical Research, and of such editors as wrote to it, is that no torment is too frightful, no agony too prolonged, to be inflicted in the name of science.'

62 'Our entire nation is harmed, as surely harmed as by radioactive fallout ... by cruelty that has the appearance of social sanction and legal blessing.'

60 'Research in psychology has produced some of the most revolting and least defensible cruelties ...'

226 'At Cornell University researchers destroyed the sight, hearing and sense of smell in cats, and then for a period of ten years applied such stimuli as (a) electrical shocks delivered via a metal grid covering the floor, (b) blows on the face with a plastic flyswatter, and (c) pinching the tip of the tail.'

311 'I recently asked a young physician how the newer medical students can judge the need for sedatives if the dog has been "devocalized" as the scientists phrase it. His answer was startling. He said: "It is the prevalent attitude in medical schools now that dogs can't feel pain—dogs do not suffer." The prevalent attitude: meaning, in the simplest terms, that medical students are

encouraged to believe that drugs to relieve the animals' pain are not required ... they cannot feel it. That theory is an astounding example of scientific hypocrisy. If a research worker can seriously reject the idea that animals suffer, how dependable are his conclusions from the results of his experiments? ... Without a basic understanding of pain, its causes and its significance, what kind of doctors are being turned out by the medical schools today?'

264 'While talking to the doctor in charge, I asked him if sedation was used to ease the sufferings of animals in prolonged painful experiments. He raised his eyebrows and said: "Suffering – science has not proved yet that animals suffer. To think they suffer is anthropomorphism. We believe that any reflex or reaction is instinct, and is not induced by a sensation of pain."* One of the employees in that institution resigned, because he could not bear to hear the animals cry ... This same doctor and some of the dealers are members of the animal-care panel, which is supposed to develop standards for the care of laboratory animals.'

312 'Most of the suffering never comes to light. The only people who know about it are those who are responsible for it.'

253 'But the dog was in a basement so only we could hear, and I was there to suffocate the screams ... The dog visibly resisted crying out – until she could no longer bear the pain ... Maybe you – or you – can listen to a dog scream her heart out in a basement room; but if you can, your morals, sensitivity, and principles have rotted like the flesh of those wounds, and there can be no God in your world.'

* * *

No God. But there are beautiful chapels in some of these institutions.

Chapels and no God? What purpose do they serve? It may be that those who come to them are seeking reassurance. Perhaps

* See, ante p. 35.

they have heard, or intuitively know, that 'Cruelty is the greatest of sins, and the furthest from redemption.' They have grown anxious, and they would like to be reassured. In some research laboratories in Japan, where vivisection is even more merciless, there are little shrines where scientists assemble once a year to propitiate the spirits of the animals they have 'sacrificed'. The chapels are a counterpart of these shrines, and both serve the needs of minds that are uneasy – in the West from a sense of guilt, and in the East from a fear of being haunted. But if animals do have souls, they are not malicious. It is not they who will haunt us, but indelible memories that no visit to an empty chapel will erase – memories of a dog screaming, strapped to a board in a basement-room, in a world where there is no God.

Such things cry vengeance on the human race.

A number of witnesses drew attention to what might be termed standardized atrocities – to procedures, that is to say, that require elaborate machines. The presumption that such 'experiments' will be indefinitely repeated rests on the nature of the equipment they entail. Laboratories are not museums. If they find money and room for an expensive apparatus, it is there to be used.

One of the machines exhibited at these hearings was the Noble-Collip Drum. This was invented about the year 1941, by Dr R. L. Noble, a Canadian, and Dr J. B. Collip, a Fellow of the Royal Society. Its purpose is to produce traumatic shock in small animals, such as hamsters and guinea-pigs, although it could be adapted to larger ones. They are not anaesthetized, their feet are usually taped together, and they are placed inside the drum which is rotated by an electric motor. The interior is fitted with steel projections, so that at each revolution the animals are carried to the top of the drum and then dropped. In one experiment which the inventors describe, the animals were 'drummed' to death, observations being made at each hundred revolutions. Among the injuries produced by 'drumming' are fractured skulls, bruised livers, and engorgement of the bowels, kidneys, lungs and stomach; and the verb 'to drum', in this sense has become part of the language of biomedical research.

Another apparatus shown to the Committee was the Blalock Press. This was invented in 1942, by Dr Alfred Blalock of John Hopkins University. Its purpose is to produce experimental shock in dogs, by crushing the limbs without breaking the bones. The hind legs are fixed in the press, which can be calibrated to exert pressures up to five thousand pounds per square inch. After several hours, the flesh is crushed to a pulp, while the bones remain unbroken. One group of researchers crushed four hundred dogs in the Blalock Press. Most died in extreme pain within five to twelve hours of release, some survived for twenty-four hours, and none was given any sedation. The Humane Society of the United States, in a study of scientific periodicals, found reports of forty-three investigations, involving more than four thousand dogs, which made use of the Blalock Press.

Even if there were no other evidence, this would be enough to show that science and savagery are not incompatible. Much thought has gone into the design of such equipment; its manufacture is expensive; it is made for use; and its employment is the professional occupation of men and women who, in the scientific sense, are among the most highly educated in the modern world. Shall society not pay for this? We think not, because we have dismissed the concept of a wider justice. But we may be wrong.

Let us take one last example of repetitive atrocity – experimental burns. Animals have been subjected to them for at least a hundred years; and yet it has been thought necessary to construct a special fire-proof room at Harvard University where experimental burns can be inflicted without risk of setting the building on fire. No doubt this was a wise precaution; but such regressions into barbarism could set our universities on fire in another and a deeper sense. A point that was well made at these hearings was that many students come from homes where animals are loved, and that they arrive at their colleges more humane, and therefore more moral, than they leave them. They have acquired knowledge when they leave, but at the expense of those qualities without which the power conferred by knowledge will be misused.

This is not education, it is corruption. From the places where we have traditionally sought – and hitherto found – civilization and light, a new barbarism is being spread. If chancellors and presidents had retained a sense of the civilizing function of their universities, they would not have forgotten that such cruelties have been condemned by the majority of the most illustrious men and women of the last two hundred years. Those who passed this adverse judgment were the creators of our culture. And if today, in the very places where that culture should be fostered, their voices are unheard, we are entering a new dark age; and that wider justice, in which we do not believe, will therein be meted out to us.

The Humane Society of the United States was represented at these hearings by Mr Fred Myers, and our final quotation is a passage from his masterly address. It deals particularly with this ominous happening – that the light of the academic world is being dimmed:

'I have myself, in the last five years, visited more than forty of the largest and best-known animal-using laboratories in the United States. I have seen and studied their animal-cages, their records, their procedures, their personnel. I have been the immediate supervisor of a staff of investigators of the Humane Society of the United States who have spent an aggregate of several years working inside medical school laboratories as animal caretakers and laboratory technicians.

'In the course of this work and study of the subject I have seen tens of thousands of animals so inhumanely housed and cared for that the condition itself constitutes cruelty. At Johns Hopkins University I have seen closely caged dogs suffering from advanced bleeding mange, without treatment. At Georgetown University I have seen a German Shepherd dog confined in a basement cage so small that the animal could not stand erect. At Marquette University I have seen forty or fifty dogs locked up in rows and tiers of small cages with no runway or exercise space available at any time for any of the animals. At Tulane University we found cats confined in cages suspended from the ceiling, with the wire mesh of the cage floors so widely spaced that the cats could not walk, stand, or lie down in a normal manner. At New York University I walked for several hours, on a weekend, through several floors of caged dogs, cats, monkeys, rats, rabbits, sheep and other animals, scores of them wearing the bandages of major surgery, and many of them obviously desperately ill, without ever encountering any doctor, veterinarian, caretaker, or even a building janitor. The Overholzer Thoracic Clinic, in Massachusetts, has kept animals convalescing from surgery in such pigsty conditions that a Massachusetts court, on complaint of the Massachusetts SPCA, returned a verdict of illegal cruelty.

'At Loma Linda University, in California, unlicensed kennel men have performed "debarking" surgery on dogs. In the Children's Hospital in Cincinnati one of our investigators found small rhesus monkeys chained by their necks inside steel cages so small that the animals could barely move. Kennel men at Leland Stanford University habitually, while we had an investigator working there, turned both hot and cold hose water on sick animals while washing their cages, rather than undertake the labor of cleaning by hand...

'I have myself seen mere technicians – men with no academic degrees and with no pretence at professional qualifications – performing the work of a surgeon in a laboratory of the National Institutes of Health. I have seen a live and fully conscious dog, with an open incision into the thoracic and abdominal cavity, lying on the concrete floor of a corridor in that same laboratory, writhing deperately but unable to rise, while a dozen or more men and women passed without so much as a sideways glance...

'I indict Harvard University, Northwestern University,

Chicago University, Creighton University, the University of Pittsberg, the National Institutes of Health, Western Reserve University – every one of which I know to have been guilty of neglect and mistreatment of animals. I can and will supply details to any extent that this committee desires.'

Never has there been such an indictment of long-honoured institutions; and seldom, one may think, has any Committee of Congress listened to such bitter words; but these accusations are just and due. It is time for anger; time to strip cruelty of urbane deceit; time to expose the callous careerists who are expectant of honours and deserving of disgrace; it is time – or it will be too late – for humane values in science. If these are not imposed, and seen to be respected, there will be a revulsion from science itself; and only those who have been enlightened by science, who appreciate and love it, can comprehend that tragedy.

Many years ago, at the beginning of the century, George Gissing had such a presentiment. It seemed eccentric then, if not absurd. It does not seem so now. 'I hate and fear science,' Gissing wrote, 'because of my conviction that, for long to come if not for ever, it will be the remorseless enemy of mankind. I see it destroying all simplicity and gentleness of life, all the beauty of the world; I see it restoring barbarism under a mask of civilization; I see it darkening men's minds and hardening their hearts; I see it bringing a time of vast conflicts, which will pale into insignificance "the thousand wars of old", and, as likely as not, will whelm the laborious advances of mankind in blood-drenched chaos.'*

Gissing had seen, in prophetic imagination, the dark face of science; but one should not lose distinction in one's hates, and he seems not to have perceived its face of light. It must, therefore, be said again that a rational understanding of the world could be among the purest and deepest of our joys, and that even if the catastrophy he foresaw should happen, it would be wrong to hate

* George Gissing: *The Private Papers of Henry Ryecroft*, Everyman ed., p. 204.

science. What is to be hated and feared is the shadow-side of man made more deadly by scientific knowledge, and a callous – at its worst, sadistic – curiosity that our society has been persuaded to accept, and even to acclaim.

On what grounds do we assert the right to torture? Is it due to us because we are immortal souls? But love, loyalty and self-sacrifice are the qualities of immortality – and we find these qualities in at least some of the creatures we torment. Is it due to us, then, because our brains are better? It is not certain that they always are. The dolphin's brain is larger and more elaborate than ours; and from the anatomical standpoint, it would seem to be superior. Is it, then, because we use our brains to finer issues? Or is it simply because we have the power?

In his book, *Man and Dolphin*, Dr J. C. Lilly* describes his attempts to discover why the dolphin has so large a brain, and what it does with it. To answer these questions he had recourse to a method that had been worked out on other animals, chiefly monkeys. The monkey is restrained in a steel chair, and a short length of metal tubing is hammered into the skull so that it just penetrates the brain-cavity. Through this 'sleeve' an electrode is thrust gradually into the brain itself, and observations are made at each millimetre of its advance. In this way, while the monkey is fully conscious, the electrical potentials given off at varying depths can be measured, and each area can be stimulated by passing a current through the electrode. By dint of patience, the brain can thus be 'mapped'; and the behaviour of its owner may even be controlled.

This could be done to the human brain – either by a well-meaning psychiatrist or by an insane dictator – and so it is possible to claim that the invention of this technique may be of benefit to man. But when Dr Lilly applied it to the dolphins, he had a more surprising end in view. He tells us – and he is entirely

---

* Not to be confused with Dr Harry R. Lillie, author of *The Path Through Penguin City*.

serious – that if we can learn to communicate with the dolphins, the experience may be of value when, in the course of exploring space, we make our first encounter with extra-terrestrial beings. This seems like the point at which science passes into science-fiction. But the doctor is writing as a scientist, and he may be correct. It is therefore permissible to speculate a little further. Let us suppose that the 'beings' we encounter are more clever and powerful than we are, but have the same moral standards as ourselves. In that case, they will conquer the earth; and when they have done so, they will say to us: 'We are more advanced than you, and we are of far greater cosmic importance; but there are still some things we do not know. We shall have to make experiments; and as you are the most suitable subject, we shall make them on you. We know you will agree to the rightness of this; because you have always said that it is entirely ethical for a higher species to experiment on a lower one, if it can discover something that may be of value to itself.'

When this does happen, we shall see a flaw in the argument very quickly; but we shall be in no condition to debate the matter then. When we are taken by our conquerors to our own laboratories, when we are traumatized in the Noble-Collip Drum, when our limbs are crushed in the Blalock Press, when we are restrained in the monkey-chair while our brains are accurately mapped, all we shall be able to do, unless we have been de-voiced as we now debark our laboratory dogs, will be to scream, 'You devils!' And, at last, we shall know ourselves.

Appendix

EXTRACTS FROM TWO ADDRESSES

BY PROFESSOR DR S. T. AYGÜN
University of Ankara

Delivered at the Congress of the World Coalition Against Vivisection, Amsterdam, 1967, and at the Inaugural Meeting of the International Association against Painful Experiments on Animals, London, 1969.*

Amsterdam, 1967

The subject I should like to talk about has the title, *Cell and Tissue Cultures and their Use as an Alternative to Vivisection*.

I call those animal-experiments vivisection that cause animals distress, pain, or damage to health.

I should like to distinguish between three fields of vivisection:

(1) Medico-biological investigation and drug manufacture;
(2) Physiological teaching and demonstration purposes;
(3) Teaching and laboratory practice for students of Zoology and Natural Sciences.

Considering these three points in the light of present-day scientific demands and possibilities, and leaving aside humanitarian factors, *there is no need for vivisection*. In medicine, there are now other, more humane ways, which can fully satisfy all relevant demands.

* Full texts may be obtained from the International Association Against Painful Experiments on Animals, 51 Harley Street, London, W.1.

Where physiology and surgery are concerned, thousands of experiments have been carried out in the past so that models, films, and video-tapes can be used for training students.

For other medical work there are many other possibilities which do not violate the humanitarian feelings expected of a civilized society.

Medicine is, of course, a humanitarian study. For a doctor the first and foremost consideration must be the feeling of humanity. Vivisection, however, dulls feelings of compassion for living creatures in the young student. This is a fatal fact which cannot be tolerated ... The relationship between man and animal and between all living creatures must be such that the place and value of each in nature is seen and *respected*. Man with his reason, in particular, must be aware of his duty to protect the weaker members in nature. To my mind, animal protection is a moral duty. Unfortunately, the animal is still treated in our society as a mere object. A truly cultured person must and does, however, feel the moral duty of compassion. Without this moral duty towards the living, a genuine civilization is impossible.

What do we understand by cell and tissue cultures?

We understand by this the cultivation of normal or neoplastic (cancerous) tissues and cells obtained from warm-blooded or cold-blooded animals, invertebrates and plants by biopsy, surgical operation or section, from slaughterhouses, or poultry or mammalian embryos or foetuses, fruit-skins, or parts of plants. Eggs of marine invertebrates, and animal or vegetable unicellular organisms are also used. These are kept alive and bred in artificial nutritive media, not in animal, human or plant bodies.

The history of the tissue and cell culture method is fairly old. Initially, people were curious to see whether parts of organs could be kept alive outside the body. Many lines of investigation have led to today's state of advance.

Real progress will be achieved in medical research when it is commonly accepted that therapeutic material should be tested, not on animals, but on human cell tissue in vitro.

Animal experiments have many disadvantages compared to cell cultures.

* * *

London, 1969

Despite the great shortcomings of animal experiments they have grown rapidly, and have reached such astronomic proportions that in the history of medicine there has never been so much vivisection as there is today.

Among the experimenters using animals, virologists come at the top of the list; they are followed by pharmacologists, toxicologists, and the drug industries. Nowadays, organ-transplantation experimentation has been rapidly growing too.

I am among the first virologists to have conducted research by using tissue-culture techniques, and I have done thousands of experiments in this field. Today we have strong evidence to suggest that in virology, by using this technique, all the problems can be solved.

However, the possible use of cell-culture systems are ignored by most pharmacologists, toxicologists, and those engaged in the drug industry. From this standpoint, I must urge that their potentialities should be explored and examined by the drug companies and other concerned institutions.

On this problem the following questions have frequently been put to me:

(1) Could the cultured cells really be substituted for living animals and human subjects?
(2) Could the results obtained by cell, tissue and organ culture methods be applied to human beings or animals without animal experimentation?
(3) Can drug testing on the tissue cultures be accepted as a final result without using experimental animals?

(4) Could the vaccines be manufactured directly without being tested on experimental animals?

Almost every human tissue and organ can be grown in culture. Fragments of human tissues, both normal and diseased, obtainable from hospital operating rooms, can be used. They can be cultivated as growing and functioning cell cultures. They can also be obtained from some firms that actually grow cell cultures for use by research scientists.

Cells cultivated from human organs not only live and grow, but also function as they did when they were in a human body; for example, heart cells continue to *beat*, muscle cells to *pulsate*, brain cells to *rotate* and to react to the electroencephalogram, reticuloendothelial system cells to *produce antibodies and hormones*, etc., in cell cultures.

The study of drug action on tissue culture gives us very interesting results.

Various drugs in various concentrations were tested; for example, on beating heart cells, some experiments made the cells beat more rapidly, some slowed down the heart beat, and some stopped it altogether. This experiment showed that cell culture derived from the human heart functioned as well as the heart of a living organ.

I can point out that the advantage of testing drugs on tissue culture is that direct effects can be seen without any variables. If variables are desired, these can be introduced, and this is the basis of controlled experimentation.

I am working now with great energy to establish by a new method the use of tissue culture as a homogeneous cellular therapy for the treatment of some organ diseases which are not curable with drugs or by other means. This specific treatment is based on the cultivation of cells taken from the human foetus. Such cultivated cells have the capacity to arrive in the homologous organs in the human body when they have been injected intramuscularly or subcutaneously. Moreover they have a tendency to settle down and multiply rapidly in the new host organ and carry away the old degenerated cells so the organ will be renewed and recover itself. This kind of cellular therapy could replace most of the organ transplantation, and can be considered as an injection-implantation of homologous specific therapy.

The public look on an organ transplant as a cure for an incurable disease rather than what it is in reality. They do not know how many animals have suffered in these experiments in the laboratories, or realize that, in fact, it is not really surgery for human benefit. The only organ transplantation which is really worthwhile is corneal transplantation; and it should be added that only by the administration of dangerous and crippling drugs like the antilymphocytic and antileucocytic drugs are transplants likely to survive.

I have to add one thing to my talk. In order to pass from the present medical and biological experiments on animals to the alternative methods, we must increase the number of our laboratory experiments to demonstrate the applicabilities of tissue culture systems. If we could spend on tissue culture research only one fifth of the money which has been invested in experiments on animals, we could in a very short time obtain more practical results from the application of these alternative techniques. This is a subject to which we have to attach a great deal of importance.

Like most of you, I have been working many years in numerous associations for the protection of animals against cruelty. I have attended many conferences and meetings devoted to the protection of animals from vivisection. I must confess that we have not made any striking progress. I believe the reason for the lack of success is that our work has been mostly theoretical, and that we have been doing the work separately. Narrow concepts have hindered the progress of the anti-vivisection movement.

Our hope is now turned towards *The International Association against Painful Experiments on Animals,* the purpose of which will be to organize united progress towards the eradication of experiments on living animals. Thank you all for listening to my talk with such great patience.

Index

Allenby, Field-Marshal Lord, 155
Animal Defence and Anti-Vivisection Society, 63, 118, 122
Association for the Advancement of Medicine by Research, 75–6, 130
Aygün, Professor S. T., 198–203

Bayliss, Professor, 35, 54–6
Bergner, Rudolf, 99
Bernard, Claude, 18, 22, 46
Besant, Annie, 91
Blalock, Dr Alfred, 192
Brandt, Professor Karl, 158, 161
British Medical Journal, The, 76
British Union for the Abolition of Vivisection, foundation of, 49; 80, 85; Hadwen president of, 87; 124
Brown Dog, The 35, 53, Chapter V
Browning, Robert, 25

Carlyle, Thomas, 25
Church, Sir William, 68
Churchill, Sir Winston, 172
Cobbe, Frances, defended by Shaw, 25; quarrel with Coleridge, 48–49; resignation of, 51; Hadwen chosen by, 85–7; 122; quoted, 156; 171
Coleridge, Lord Chief Justice, 51
Coleridge, The Hon. Stephen, visited by Louise Lind-af-Hageby, 47; Chapter IV; evidence of, 69–77; 80, 119–20, 130
Collins, Sir William, 68
Collip, Dr J. B., 191
Conan Doyle, Sir Arthur, 120
Conti, Dr Commissioner of State for Public Health, 158, 164–6

Clynes, J. R., 95, 127–32

Daily Graphic, The, 63
Daily News, The, 56–7, 58, 63
Darwin, Charles, 106
Deignton, Kate, 99–101
Douglas Hume, Ethel, 112–14
Dowding, Air Chief Marshal Lord, 130, 173–7

Fischer, Dr Fritz, 162–4
Fletcher-Moulton, Sir John, 68
Ford, Edward, 59–60
Ford, Margaret, 118
Forster, Professor Paul, 95
French, Field-Marshal Sir John, 114
Fussy, 52

Galsworthy, John, 107–09, 133–5
Gaskell, Walter, 68
Gebhardt, Dr Karl, 158, 162–4
Gissing, George, 195–6
Gladstone, William, 52
Goethe, Johann Wolfgang von, 103–04

Haber, Professor, 115–17
Haddington, Eleventh Earl of, 121
Hadwen, Walter Robert, 49, Chapter VII, 96, 112
Haig, Field-Marshal Sir Douglas, 116
Hamilton and Brandon, Nina Duchess of, 92, 118, 121
Hardy, Thomas, 107
Henderson, Arthur, 95, 127
Hirt, Professor August, 166, 168–71
Hoggan, Dr George, 122
Horsley, Professor Sir Victor, 25–6

INDEX

Hugo, Victor, 104–07
Huxley, Aldous, 22, 143

Independent, The, 20–1
International Association against Painful Experiments on Animals, The, 180, 198, 203
Irving, Sir Henry, 52
Ivory, Netta, 121

Jung, Professor C. G., 46

Kekewich, Sir George, 91
Kingsford, Anna, 91, 139
Knight, Professor G. Wilson, 146
Kramer, Joseph, 169–70

Landor, Walter Savage, 147
Lawson Tait Memorial Trust, 124
Leffingwell, Albert, 18–20, 43–5, 73–4
Lilly, Dr J. C., 196–7
Lind-af-Hageby, Emilie Louise Augusta, Chapter II, 69, Congress organized by, 89–94; 118, 121
Linnean Society, The, 109
Lister, Joseph First Baron, 33
Littlewood, Sir Sidney, 177–9
London Anti-Vivisection Society, 24

Macdonald, Ramsay, 95, 127
MacGregor, Alasdair Alpin, 118–19
Magendie, François, 44
Manning, Cardinal, 51
Medical Research Council, The, 128–32
Metcalfe, Harvey, 120–2
Millevoye, Lucien, 93
Morning Post, The, 63
Mrugrowski, Dr Joachim, 159
Munro, The Rev. R. D., 100–01
Myers, F., 193–5

National Anti-Vivisection Society, The, Shaw's address to, 24–5; Coleridge Hon. Sec. of, 48; new policy of, 50; 58, 85, 124
Newman, Cardinal, 51

Nisbet, A. C. T., 121
Noble, Dr R. L., 191

Paget, Sir Stephen, 92, 94
Pasteur Institute, The, 31–2
Powys, J. C., Chapters XIII & XIV
Pythagoras, 103

Quidde, Professor, 97–8

Rascher, Dr. Sigmund, 160–1
Rhadamanthus, 151–2
Robert Koch Institute, The, 164
Rose, Professor Gerhardt, 158, 164, 166
Rostock, Professor Paul, 158
Royal Commissions of Inquiry into Experiments on Animals (1875), 74, 129–30; (1906–1912) Chapter VI
Royal Society for the Prevention of Cruelty to Animals, 67, 179
Ruff, Dr Seigfried, 158
Ruskin, John, 25

Sade, Marquis de, 141, 147–9
Schartau, Liesa Katrina, Chapter II
Scottish Society for the Prevention of Vivisection, The, 120–1, 124
Searle, Dr George F. C., 122–3, 153
Shaftesbury, Seventh Earl of, 49, 100, 122, 132
Shaw, George Bernard, 20, Chapter II, quoted, 77–8; 91; reply to Wells, 135–6; 158, 171
Slosson, Professor E. E., 20–1
Snowden, Philip, 95, 127
Somers, Eighth Baron, 176
Standard, The, 61
Star, The, 62
Starling, Professor Ernest, 55, 57
Stricker, Professor Simon, 45
Sunday Express, The, 135–6

Taliesin, 151–4
Taylor, Brig. General Telford, 157–8
Tennyson, Alfred Lord, 25, 52
Times, The, 17, 92

Verulam Review, The, 67–8
Victoria, Queen, 17, 33, 132

Wagner, Richard, 106–07
Wallace, Alfred Russel, 109–10, 158
Wells, H. G., 135–6
Wilberforce, Archdeacon, 94
Wilcox, Ella Wheeler, 94

Wilde, Oscar, 52
William II of Prussia and German Emperor, 17, 18
Woodward, Anna Louise, 68
World League against Vivisection, 89, 94 et seq.

Zoophilist, The, 49–50